GROW OLD ALONG WITH ME

Reflections on Aging in a Christian Retirement Community

GROW OLD ALONG WITH ME

Reflections on Aging in a Christian Retirement Community

By

Wesley F. Stevens

Quotations at the beginning of chapters have been taken, for the most part, from *Familiar Quotations* by John Bartlett, Fourteenth Edition, Emily Morison Beck, Editor (Little, Brown & Company: Boston, 1968). This includes two quotations from William Shakespeare that are located and identified as such within the text. The quote beginning Chapter Six, "Receiving the Gifts", is reprinted by permission from the *Christian Century*, December 21-28, 1988, "From a God We Hardly Knew," by William H. Willimon. Quotations from hymns are taken from *The Methodist Hymnal* (Nashville, The Methodist Publishing House, 1966). Quotations from the Bible, unless otherwise noted, are from the Revised Standard Version of the Bible (New York, Thomas Nelson & Sons, 1952).

Holly Hall
8304 Knight Road
Houston, Texas 77054

Companion Press
P.O. Box 351
Shippensburg, PA 17257

ISBN 1-56043-436-8

For Worldwide Distribution
Printed in the U.S.A.

Contents

Foreword

Over the last several decades, continuing care retirement communities in the United States have grown at an exponential rate. The percentage of those with religious connections has, however, decreased. Fewer and fewer religious institutions are committing time and resources to caring for older persons at a time when more and more are looking for security and the assurance that they will be cared for should they become frail and dependent on others. Holly Hall Retirement Community in Houston, Texas, is an exception to the rule. Here, there is not only a connection to long-honored religious values, but there is a clear commitment to finding ways of expressing them in and around the lives of those for whom the community exists.

Wes Stevens, in *Grow Old Along With Me*, tells his story of relating to, caring for and sharing in the drama of retirement and nursing home living in a Christian atmosphere. As the Administrator of Holly Hall for more than two decades, he has learned to let the residents be his mentors. Early in the book he expresses it well: "It is enough to be accepting, to listen carefully and to absorb as much of their wisdom as possible." He has allowed them to teach him that, while change is the one constant in life, one's faith provides the "bulwark against the often frightening prospect of change."

In Chapter Five, a theology of grace and love springs forth as the reader is challenged to remember that God accepts us unconditionally and that this is the case regardless of one's human condition. This follows a poignant message contained in the previous chapter which stresses that a person has value and worth regardless of his physical and mental state, and that it is the responsibility of everyone (staff and families) to pursue a meaningful existence. More specifically, what is implied is that unconditional acceptance is a kind of holy love which is needed not only by the one for whom care is provided, but also for the caregiver who provides it.

Part I is brought to a close with a comforting reminder that those who give will receive. How true that is. Persons who visit, work with, love and care for others are most definitely the ones who reap the rewards, the benefits. How wrong it is to think that when we visit a frail older person we are performing an act of ministry. In fact, it is often the person we visit who does the blessing. It is the visitor, not just the visited, who experiences God's love and affection.

Part II provides glimpses of living in a retirement community characterized by multiple levels of care. The illustrations and examples bring alive the trials and tribulations, the joys and frustrations of community life. The constant key to survival and meaningful existence is, however, faith. This is the glue which holds the community and everyone in it together. When Dr. Stevens begins to share his own moments of experiential and theological learning, especially those based on his spending the weekend in the nursing home unit as a patient, the story really comes to life. Wes Stevens puts himself in the midst of those for whom he cares. Indeed, for a weekend, he becomes one of them. How fitting that he chose Good Friday to begin the experience and Easter Day to complete it. On Friday he was a student, yet on Sunday he was your teacher and mine.

Perhaps this is the message Wes Stevens offers us: Jesus had to leave the crowd in order to touch the leper. He did this to remind us that the leper has value and worth—and that what we do unto others is what we do unto Him. It is when we avoid the leper that we stray from our faith. Yes, acceptance is the key. An unconditional kind of love is what we are asked to share with others. This is the spirit of Holly Hall and it is captured in this book.

David B. Oliver Ph. D., Vice President
Rehabilitation, Chronic and Long-Term Care Services, Heartland Centre,
St. Joseph, Missouri

Dedicated to all who have served as President of the Holly Hall Board of Directors

Preface

"Growing old is no picnic, but considering the alternative I think I'll stick around awhile." I have forgotten who made that statement. It probably was one of the residents at Holly Hall, the Christian Retirement Community in Houston, Texas, where I live and work as the Administrator.

Growing into the last years of life does have its problems and frustrations, but it also can be a time of quiet contentment and personal enrichment. It has been my pleasure through the years to see how many people have the capacity to live through the ups and downs of old age with keen minds and active bodies. Their reasoned judgments and wholesome activities characterize them as people who have a purpose in life and who are determined to make the best of the days that remain to them.

Grow Old Along With Me! is written to help set the record straight about the last years of life for which, as Browning said, "the first were made." Those who are considering a move to a retirement community may find these thoughts of some value. Those aspiring to volunteer service to meet the needs of older people can be included as potential readers, as well as those who have entered, or who contemplate entering, any of the helping professions involved with geriatrics. Adult children may discover something in these pages that will help them with the problems of taking care of their aging parents. It is my hope that ministers will take the time to read it. This message is also for those who are interested in knowing what it is like, on a daily basis, to assist individuals in community who have lived far longer than the biblical "three score and ten" years. It especially is for God's pilgrim people (anywhere and of any age) who joyfully move through life as if they indeed are in the "last days."

I want to acknowledge the support I receive from my mother-in-law, Mrs. William A. Andel, Sr., and the assistance I receive from Mrs. Elaine Geist, Assistant Administrator, whose commitment to the Christian faith makes her an invaluable associate in the process of ministry to, for and with the residents of Holly Hall.

I am thankful for the life and work of Dr. W. Paul Jones, professor of philosophical theology and, at the time I entered the Doctor of Ministry program, director of doctoral studies at St. Paul School of Theology, Kansas City, Missouri. I was moved by his teaching and friendship toward a greater flexibility and openness, thereby prompting the renewal of a writing impulse that was first experienced during my early days at

Holly Hall. I want to acknowledge, as well, the important contribution to my learning endeavor of Dr. David Oliver who, at the time, occupied the Poppele Chair of Gerontology at St. Paul. His role as the primary faculty consultant for my studies enabled me to reestablish my commitment to Christian ministry in the setting with which I am most familiar.

The residents of Holly Hall deserve special mention. Without them this story would not be told. They inspire and inform in ways that I will try to convey in these pages. Those who have passed through the numbered corridors will live on in my memory even as the current residents are establishing their own place in Holly Hall history.

Finally, I want to note the importance to me of my wife, Marilyn, and our two grown-up children, Carolyn and Van. Each brings something special to my life even as they, in consort, help to lighten my occasionally ponderous disposition. We have grown older and wiser through our relationships with those who always will be "ahead of us."

Wesley F. Stevens

Introduction

Chapter One sets the stage for all that follows by looking at the meaning of life from the perspective of those who are growing old. It examines how living the Christian faith relates to the fulfillment of life at every point of the journey and how older people need the acceptance of those who do not take them for granted. It speaks to the need for compassion and understanding in those who are entrusted with the special task of serving the needs of this age group, and it asks that we avoid judgments about older persons based on many of the unfortunate stereotypes that our society has placed upon them.

Chapter 1

Where Does It All Begin?

The child is father of the man.
—William Wordsworth

Endings are always tied to beginnings. It is impossible to talk about the end of the life cycle without acknowledging the beginning and knowing something of the pattern of existence in between. Those who would learn of the elderly and their needs must first learn of life itself. To know what it is like to be seventy-five years of age is either to know yourself if you have reached that mark or to know someone who has. Even then, such knowledge is limited by one's own narrow vision of self and others. What it is like, therefore, to be a certain age is an individual matter and depends not so much on present circumstances as it does on the complete package of influences that have helped to shape each life from the very beginning.

The minute we enter into life we begin the process of growth and maturation that will lead, barring early death, to what is known as old age. When children look at those who have lived for many years and think to themselves how long it takes for Christmas to come each year, they cannot imagine ever being old. For the youth who longs to be free from parental restrictions, the teen years seem to stretch on forever. Even the approach of the difficult middle years is unconvincing to many who blithely assume that they still have a long way to go. However, it is in this range of years that some uneasiness begins to set in over the swift accumulation of birthdays. We see many ridiculous attempts to preserve a youthful image. Prompted by the advertising industry's concept of the strong, beautiful and healthy which flashes before us, there are many different ways we try to hide what the over-forty years are doing to us. A number of people in this age group become depressed because their education and experience have not brought them to the place where their sights had been set. They may have children to educate and aging parents to assist. They may begin to doubt the wisdom of earlier influences and decisions. It is truly the grace of God that enables a triumphant emergence through these middle age crises to a wholesome and happy existence later on down the line. When one has known a number of older people who have made it through these years successfully, there is reason to be optimistic about life past seventy.

We are indeed fearfully and wonderfully made. We are a complex jumble of psychological and physical properties. Much of what we are can be traced to our origins. Certain traits are inherited; certain physical characteristics are determined from the beginning by genes and chromosomes. Behavior traits are often passed on from parents to their children. But our faith teaches us that we also are children of God, and most of us have the opportunity to accept that fact and to live accordingly. We should never offer excuses for our failure or lack of personal initiative, saying, "There is nothing I can do; I was just made that way." Unfortunately, God is blamed for what, in a great many people, is nothing more than a cultivated laziness. These people have made a habit of avoiding or ignoring responsibility for their actions.

While those who have reached the seventieth year of their lives cannot truthfully deny the years, they may still push aside thoughts of their own end by comparing themselves (favorably, of course) to others who are their own age. They may also exalt their own endurance by looking over the obituary notices in the daily newspaper and observing how many younger ones have preceded them in death. Not all of these attitudes and devices are unhealthy. To indulge in them does not mean that one cannot accept the reality of death. It means, for the majority of healthy individuals, that the urge to live is a strong one. It means that our survival instincts cause us to react to the threat of non-being in various ways, most of which are acceptable to God and our human companions.

So every life is a drama, a story of sunshine and of shadow, of beginnings and endings, of joy and sorrow. In the New Testament sense, life begins (or is renewed) as the grace of God enables faith to overcome the dreary wasteland of sin and when we are no longer defeated in spirit by pain, sorrow and a variety of disappointments.

Life begins (or is renewed) at any age when we learn to accept it as a gift. This acceptance can, in some instances, be defined as a religious experience. It may, from time to time, require reaffirmation. These times of renewal, or recovery of hope, tend to make all things seem fresh and new. They come just as surely to those who have lived for many years as they do to those whose years are few in number. Actually, it is not unreasonable to assume that it is when the visions of youth are joined with the mature judgments of the later years that a greater sense of fulfillment is at last achieved. However, what children receive from their parents and other adults early in life often predetermines whether or not they will have any dreams left over for old age. Therefore, it is very important that parents guide their children with wisdom and loving concern. Children need the freedom to experiment and to make excursions into the land of make believe. We must give them permission to be unique, responsible individuals. This does not mean, of course, allowing them to do things that are destructive and disrespectful. We want people, late in life, to be free of the heavy hand of harshly imposed restrictions placed upon them as children. It is unfortunate that some older people have had their lives so closely managed that they must rely solely upon certain family members or friends to make all of their decisions for them. They usually expect these same ones to offer them approval and acceptance.

The question often is asked, "Why do the elderly act as they do?" More correctly, it should be asked, "Why does any particular individual behave as he does?" It all started somewhere. Elderly people may possess certain similar characteristics because of physical impairment, the gradual loss of friends and relatives and diminishing opportunities for personal fulfillment. Many older people are forced into a pattern of existence that they would not otherwise assume because of pressures from family members and the rejection they feel being thrust upon them by a youth-oriented culture. But it does not have to be this way. We may expect God's judgment upon us for the ways in which we have been callous, cruel or even indifferent toward persons of advanced age for whom we have any degree of responsibility. Older men and women, surely as precious in God's sight as the tiny babies they once were, often are relegated to places of abode where they are little more than "kept" by others. All too often these places, and they go by a variety of names, provide too little in the way of compassionate, understanding care. Who, then, is responsible? Certainly, the nursing homes and their personnel or individuals who keep older people in their homes should not receive all of the blame. There are quite a few good nursing and retirement homes, many caring relatives, and even friends who are performing exceptionally well under difficult circumstances. In the broader sense, all of us stand guilty of not doing as much as we could to make life less burdensome for the elders in our midst. The medical profession is just now waking up to the special understanding required in the treatment of older persons. Churches still are behind in allowing older members to maintain significant relationships in the life of the congregation. Younger people are often neglectful of members of the older generation. The government is criticized for not doing enough to help the elderly. Activist elders speak of the need (and act upon it) to help their own cause. All of us must offer the best of which we are capable, through our respective disciplines, to achieve the best results. Solutions to each crisis of human need are obtained through the cooperative work of people who approach the challenge from different directions.

If we have learned to accept the mediocre as being good enough, then we will not push for better conditions or, perhaps, even realize how they could be better. If we have let selfishness control our actions, then we are not likely to be concerned with how our resources and talents can be utilized to provide the kind of assistance that our older friends and relatives need. If, as individuals, we are insecure, then we are not likely to inspire hope and confidence in others. Such inadequacies are magnified when they relate to the care of the elderly. Rationalizations abound in this area. "It's good enough." "The family won't make trouble." "So little satisfies them." The implication may be given that other ideas and opinions are not worth consideration. The sacredness of life is rejected by these thoughts and attitudes. The Christian perspective is one that views each person as a child of God. We may speak, I think, of God sorrowing over each act of abuse or neglect that any one of these special people must endure.

Motives for serving the needs of people spontaneously emerge from love working through faith. If we are not possessed by this spirit during the years when we are especially accountable, then we can neither minister with acceptable and helping love to those who are beset by disabling circumstances of old age, nor can we hope to age gracefully ourselves. The Church, as it ministers to the whole person, uniquely qualifies to be the agent through which God works miracles of grace. Through its involvement with families, it exalts each stage of life as possessing unique blessings and opportunities.

All of this is to lay the groundwork for the chapters to come. It provides a basis for a deeper realization of the special needs of the elderly. Everything that follows will be expressed within the context of looking at life holistically. This approach avoids judgments about any individual on the basis of age or outward appearance. Through my relationship with so many who have grown old before me, I have been able to learn what influences shape their lives. When contact with older people is not as direct, or as routine, it is enough to be accepting, to listen carefully and to absorb as much of their wisdom as possible.

Acknowledging the importance of all of the years each person has lived, even though we cannot know all of the significant events of each life, makes it possible to respond with greater understanding to the needs of older persons in our ministry.

PART I

These chapters contain information, and some inside views, relating to the when, the where, the who and the how of retirement community living. It is interesting to note the changes that have occurred through the years in what congregate housing for older people is called. For example, when Holly Hall was first established, and for several years thereafter, it was known as "Holly Hall, Home for the Aged." From the late 60s into the early 80s, it was known as "Holly Hall Retirement Home." Then, with the sudden boom of retirement housing in the 80s, we started hearing the term "Continuing Care Retirement Community" (CCRC). Holly Hall, having been a pioneer in the concept of continuing care, and because of its special emphasis on the Christian aspects of service to the elderly, suddenly took on the title of "Holly Hall, A Christian Retirement Community." In order to serve the present age, it is important to reflect what we are as accurately as possible.

I have never particularly liked the term "retirement village," even though it is used, at times, in place of "retirement home" or "retirement community." It fosters images in my mind of a circle of tepees with smoke curling up from a central camp fire.

While nursing homes and intermediate care facilities, variously described as custodial care, personal care or assisted living, serve a particular level of need for elderly people, the continuing care retirement community features housing for every level of need, all the way from completely independent living to skilled nursing care. The areas of nursing care once called "Semi-Infirmary" and "Infirmary" at Holly Hall are now part of what is known as the "Health Center."

Many of the thoughts presented in Part I derive from my earliest experiences at Holly Hall. I believe they are as valid now for understanding the particular concerns of growing old as when they were first written. The greatest difference is seen in the changes in lifestyle that are the products of a more modern era. The applicant for admission today, for example, is more sensitive to conveniences and appearances than the applicant of fifteen to twenty years ago. In earlier days, the residents of Holly Hall were, as a group, more interested in the practical aspects of personal living. They did not expect to have activities planned for them. They viewed life as an endless activity in which all of their talents combined to fulfill the need for sociability and individual achievement.

Chapter 2

When to Go and Where

He that doth live at home, and learns to know God and himself, needeth no farther to go.
—Christopher Harvey

There was a time when the elderly lived in their own homes until they were no longer able to do so, and then they went to live with a family member whose living situation was best suited to care for them. They were able to maintain a fair degree of independence until then or, as happened with many, they died in their own homes. Even when the older person went to live with family members, they generally were made to feel a part of the family and quite often were accorded a place of honor because of their seniority. This acceptance and compatibility came about, in part, because the way of life in those days had not changed so much between generations. Life still moved along family lines and there were fewer sources of friction between family members. Children often ended up with essentially the same kind of life as their parents. Today, however, the nuclear family has very little contact with members of the previous generation. An accelerated pace of life has helped to break down family solidarity.

The Old Folks' Homes that were in existence to care for those who had no family, or to house those whose family had deserted them, were poor places to live, often no more than worn old houses where the physical and spiritual nourishment was inadequate and the comforts minimal. Residents were kept in these places for meager payment until death claimed them.

With the advent of government subsidies for the building and maintenance of custodial care and nursing homes, there was an emphasis on regulated standards that were supposed to insure a higher quality of care for people who could no longer live alone. These homes also sought private paying residents who could afford more than the cost of care. There is no doubt that nursing home care was substantially improved. At the same time, improved medical care, including physical and social rehabilitation, started adding years of life to the growing number of elderly people in this country. Unfortunately, however, it did not automatically follow that these years were more fruitful and happy.

How It Is Today

Even with the rapidly growing number of nursing homes and retirement communities having different levels of care, many older people still prefer to live alone or with adult children who are willing to keep them. When a dependent older person is added to the household setting, complications often arise that make life more difficult for everyone.

Actually, fewer families today are willing to take an aging parent or grandparent into their homes. Sometimes it is done with reluctance and inadequate preparation. When such is the case, there often is resentment over the limitations brought on by the presence of the older person. Very little time is spent in making that person feel as if he or she is a welcome part of family events. There may be displeasure if too much attention is given to that person by one or more family members. The aging relative, on the other hand, may be disturbed by loud noise from TV or stereo, not to mention the possibility of an amplified guitar. His or her dietary needs may not be considered and distortions and convolutions in language may create conversational confusion. In some instances, however, harmony and mutual acceptance are achieved between several generations who occupy one house. This happens only when everyone is made to feel a part of the family and is intentionally included in the planning of events and activities. Furthermore, it is possible only when each person is willing to give up something for the good of the others in genuine love and appreciation of the needs of everyone. Because this ideal is difficult to achieve, it is no wonder that older people who are still able to think and plan for themselves feel the necessity of making other living arrangements. Sometimes they are convinced of this necessity by visits in the homes of sons and daughters who have families of their own. In other situations the difficulty may be realized only after the move has been made. It is sad how often the word "unbearable" is used to describe life together in the same house.

The desperate determination of many older people to stick it out in their own homes often frustrates well-meaning sons and daughters in their objective of finding a safe and secure place for them to live. The parent or parents may view this effort as an invitation to sever the meaningful relationships of church and community that are of many years' duration. It may seem to them as if a move such as this would be a door closing upon all they cherish and not the opening to a better way of life. It may be seen in terms of independence threatened and familiar routines disturbed. It may be doing the older person a great injustice to exert pressure upon him or her to move. Each situation should be evaluated on an individual basis.

When Should a Move Be Made?

When there is much indecision over whether to stay where one has lived for a long time or to move into a retirement home, I advise remaining in the familiar environment for as long as possible. I say this even though I know that the decision to move generally is put off too long. I believe that it is important for some people to continue with comfortable, established routines that give them satisfaction even though where they are living may involve a certain amount of risk. Then, as it becomes harder for them to manage totally independent living (grocery shopping, cooking, home ownership) they should, without further delay, consider a change.

When a move is put off too long the only alternative may be admission to a nursing home. The warning signs that precede such action having to be taken are reports of forgetting to turn off the stove, failing to take medication as required, not taking a bath often enough or excessive health problems. Accomplishing such a move is an emotionally exhausting task for family members and often is accompanied by feelings of guilt and uncertainty. A move to a retirement community, by comparison, is much less painful.

When anyone asks me about the prospects of retirement home living for themselves or for a parent, I want to know the needs and expectations that are involved. I want to know the reasons an inquirer has for discussing the possibility of a move on behalf of another person. Sometimes the answers to my questions are quite negative. Sometimes, unfortunately, they are spoken out of frustration. Those who inquire for themselves often do so out of a vague uneasiness over their health or safety. A serious applicant may say, "I don't want to be put in a nursing home when I can no longer care for myself." Another may have built up a fear of falling or being robbed to the extent that she is willing to give up a home of many years. A move may be considered by someone who is energetic and independent simply because he is tired of living alone and cooking for himself. The expense of living in a large house may create the need for change. Every reason must be given serious consideration in the process of determining the best time for a retired person to think seriously about the advantages of retirement home living.

It is clear that a decision to move away from a home of many pleasant memories should not be made without careful thought and planning. On the other hand, non-profit church-related retirement communities should conduct careful admissions reviews in order to be sure that each person who is accepted is fully aware of what they are doing and can indicate, in a positive manner, that they are in favor of it.

I accept with great reluctance the application of anyone I feel has been talked into the idea that they should make a move. This does not mean that the idea should not be discussed. Actually, there is a time when it is wise to be thinking about another place to live. But sometimes family members make the mistake of trying to argue father or mother into moving somewhere else far too soon. Concern for their safety and well-being prompts them to rush the subject. Too often, they do not have enough respect for the capability of the parent to make decisions for herself/himself.

Occasionally, a son or daughter will accompany a parent (usually a mother) to my office, feeling that they have an understanding on the issue of making application. The mother, with abrupt candor, may declare that she has no intention whatsoever of moving into "one little room." I applaud the unwillingness of anyone to be persuaded into doing something that they have not had time to accept for themselves. I think that was what happened in the case of the mother and daughter who appeared by appointment in my office one day to discuss the possibility of the mother getting into Holly Hall.

It was one of those occasionally slow days in the summer when the Houston heat causes everyone to stay inside as much as possible. My visitors were cordial, the daughter being more talkative than her mother (this can be a clue as to which one has the most at stake in coming to look around). The mother listened to her daughter and made comments only on matters that did not relate specifically to what I supposed was the purpose of their visit. Her interest was aroused, for instance, when a witty statement was made concerning their background as Episcopalians.

It was decided that they would take a tour before proceeding with the application interview. This happens quite frequently. I escorted them down the hallway, telling them about all of the things the residents like about living at Holly Hall. The daughter would point to something and say, "Look, Momma, isn't that nice?" "Momma" was not what I would call disinterested, but she seemed content to reserve comment on the subject of making application for admission. When we were inside a vacant room, the daughter began indicating where they could place items of furniture. Suddenly the daughter paused and let a cry escape her lips. Quickly, her words came out. "Oh, Mother, this place is awful; you don't have to come here to live!" She embraced her mother and they both started crying. I stood helplessly in the room, wishing that I could be somewhere else. Even outside, in the "95-in-the-shade" heat, would have been fine. There wasn't anything to say. After what seemed much longer than a few minutes they both calmed down and the daughter said, "Let's get out of here!" I followed them out of the room and back toward the front door. At last, the daughter acknowledged that fact that I was still with them and offered a half-hearted apology for taking up my time. I never saw them again.

This was an interesting case of an adult child convincing her parent that a move ought to be considered and then, with a sudden rush of guilt, abandoning the idea. It made me wonder how many who face an identical problem never openly show that they are experiencing the same sort of anguish.

I may take the time, during an interview, to say some good things about retirement home living to one who appears to be a favorable candidate for admission but who is a bit frightened by the thought of having to make such a major change. I tell her (or him) how so many others have concluded, after some hesitation at first, that coming to live at Holly Hall was one of the best decisions they every made. Quite a few of our residents have thanked me later for not giving up on them while they were trying to decide what to do.

Who Should Consider a Move?

The people I like to hear talk about moving to a retirement community are those who have thought through their priorities very carefully and who have decided that such a move would give them a much more secure and worry-free life. Those who make a move of this type with the least difficulty are the ones who enjoy the company of others and who are stimulated by a variety of activities. They generally are in good physical and mental health. Family and friends are important to them. They tend to have a positive objective in mind and feel certain that they can achieve that objective in the retirement community setting. In addition, the favorable prospects may feel a need to open their lives to a larger number of people. Particular vocational experiences may enable them to render a helpful service to the community. They may grow flowers or paint or help to schedule programs. They may visit the sick or perform a variety of volunteer services. It is likely that this type of person will not be affected by gossip or complaining because she is too busy with constructive activities.

Another person who may be considered a good candidate for retirement community living is the individual who lives alone, who has reached the point where it is no longer safe to drive an automobile and who has no family upon whom to rely for transportation and assistance in emergency situations. Even for those who are in this category, it is becoming a little easier, through the growing number of home assistance programs, to stay in their own homes for a longer period of time. Church and community organizations, Meals-On-Wheels, Telephone Reassurance and Home Health Care are making it possible for older people to maintain themselves in their own homes or apartments. This is good. However, there are those in this age category who still may have feelings of insecurity and loneliness. This is especially true if family members are a great distance away. In these cases, a move to a reputable retirement community may be the best solution.

Where to Go

Where to go is often a problem for the retired person who decides that he or she should be looking for another place to live where there will be less responsibility and greater security. There are various types of retirement living centers. Many of them are designed to attract the financially able retiree. These range from high-rise apartment complexes to facilities located on attractively landscaped grounds. Many retirement communities flourish in warmer areas where people can get away from cold weather for their retirement years. These living centers often have an adjunct Health Care Unit where twenty-four hour nursing care is provided on a temporary or permanent basis. All of them have a dining area or area where residents may obtain all or a limited number of their meals. Quite a few of these retirement facilities require a substantial cash payment prior to occupancy plus a monthly maintenance fee, thereby restricting residency to those who have substantial wealth. On the other hand, there are quite a few government subsidized housing units for low-income retirees. These are relieving the growing need for retirement housing for the elderly. Churches or groups of churches often sponsor this type of housing and end up providing a certain amount of financial assistance and volunteers. It is safe to say that there is not nearly enough housing for the low and moderate income elderly.

Holly Hall

It should come as no surprise that I would want to describe Holly Hall Retirement Community as a model for anyone seeking housing for his later years. While I am affected by a natural prejudice on behalf of the place that I help to maintain, I have seen and heard enough to know that my enthusiasm is supported by the observations of a variety of knowledgeable persons who live in the greater Houston area as well as those who come to visit from other parts of the country.

Located on twenty acres donated by Mr. and Mrs. Glenn McCarthy in 1949, Holly Hall's location is ideal. It is nestled on spacious grounds two miles south of the Texas Medical Center, thus providing a very short drive to the best of medical diagnosis and treatment. This includes the advantage of being close to a growing network of services designed to inform and assist older people. Also, our location just across the street from the Astrodome Complex and close to Astroworld makes a variety of sports and entertainment events very convenient for residents and their families. Displays of fireworks, with a vast array of sparkling colors, frequently light up the night sky. It is a short distance to downtown Houston and to shopping centers. With a major traffic artery only a block away, Holly Hall is easily reached from any part of the city.

The minimum age for admission to Holly Hall is sixty-five. Application for admission must be made prior to turning eighty-five years of age. Each person, upon admission to Holly Hall, must be ambulatory, mentally capable and apparently able to adjust to a group living situation. Holly Hall is able to accept a number of qualified applicants who are not able to pay the full cost of care.

All of the buildings are single story and all of the rooms are private. Two levels of nursing care are available as residents grow older and need assistance. An attractive Activities Building provides a functional setting for many different types of programs, crafts work and parties. The beautiful chapel, built in 1958, provides a place for prayer and worship. Ministers from supporting churches conduct worship services each Sunday. The grounds are well kept and provide plenty of open space for walking and watching birds and squirrels.

Holly Hall has a long tradition of providing excellent food for the residents. A pleasant home-like atmosphere prevails in the dining areas where meals are served family style. Residents may enjoy the company of family members through special arrangements for guest meals.

Twelve cottages and three duplexes are available on the grounds for those who are fully independent. Each cottage has two bedrooms, a kitchen and a garage. Some cottage residents take the noon meal in the Dining Room on a regular basis. Others come over to the main building only to pick up their mail. Cottage residents may call the nurse on duty in the Health Center in case of an emergency.

Those who are accepted into one of the seventy single rooms at Holly Hall (which include room, board and laundry) are encouraged to think of the entire facility as their home. Even so, a move seldom is made without some anxiety. However, almost every applicant who passes the Admissions Committee review finds the problems of adjustment to living at Holly Hall minimal. For one thing, they have thought out the advantages of being here. Also, as they find peace with God, they are able to give of themselves in ways that enable personal difficulties to be kept in the background. They are not troubled with uncertainty over who will take care of them if they live into the frailty of a very old age. Indeed, their lives are enriched by engaging in useful and personally rewarding activities. It is gratifying to hear so many of the residents say, in all sincerity, "I haven't for one moment regretted my decision to come to Holly Hall."

The requirement, imposed by the Board of Directors, that an applicant must have been a resident of the Houston area for at least six months (for many years it was eighteen months) before making application, underscores a strong feeling I have that it is a wise decision to obtain retirement accommodations as close to where one has previously lived as possible. The value of having friends close at hand, a physician one knows and trusts and the good feeling that is a part of being familiar with streets and buildings is very important in the later years of life. The lure of distant, attractive retirement complexes should not entice a change unless one is accustomed to moving around and has more than a superficial knowledge of the retirement facility being considered. I suppose, for those who have spent their working years in a cold climate, the idea of sun-belt retirement might be very appealing. However, quite a few retired people have made the mistake of moving to a distant area and then, after a few years, have ended up back where they lived before.

Planning for the later yeas of one's life is important, even though it is not easy. Decisions should not be made without a great deal of practical consideration, consultation with family members and deliberate prayer. Then, "the last [part of life], for which the first was made" will not be as difficult or threatening and will, at best, present some unique opportunities for living one day at a time.

Chapter 3

The Challenge of Change

Change and decay in all around I see,
O Thou who changest not, abide with me!
—Henry F. Lyte

All of us are threatened in varying degrees by unexpected changes that come upon us. Even expected changes pose adjustment problems. At some time most of us will move, change jobs or lose a loved one. The changes brought about by these events may bring with them feelings of sorrow, anxiety, fear or disappointment. The age at which such changes occur does not make a great deal of difference. In fact, the elderly quite often are better able to accept change than young people. They have had plenty of experience.

There is one change that accompanies growing old which affects those who are married for which almost no amount of prior grief can provide adequate conditioning. It is the death of a spouse of many years. There is such emptiness, such an aching void, that it thrusts the one who remains on earth into a dark night of change from which she may never fully recover. Sometimes the experience forces the surviving spouse into changes so quickly that there is no chance to work gradually through the normal grief pattern. Even in the most favorable of circumstances, the routine of existence is changed so much that it requires an unusual amount of courage and perseverance to regain a happy and fruitful life. That process is greatly facilitated through the loving and caring support of family members and church friends.

Another more gradual and less traumatic change experienced by those who are growing old is associated with a heightened concern over the rapidly increasing cost of living. Even those who have not let finances be a particular worry to them in their younger days seem to develop a desperation over whether they will have enough money to meet various emergencies. This fear is reenforced by the stories they hear about people their age who have not had resources sufficient to take care of unexpected medical expenses. Those who work with the elderly on a daily basis occasionally witness their shock at the prices of prescription drugs and incidental necessities. These costs seem drastically high to those who do not regularly purchase such supplies.

A reduced income following retirement brings on the necessity of conserving funds and living within reasonable, debt-free limits. If older people, during their younger years, have exercised prudent care of their resources, including regularly setting aside specific amounts for savings, insurance and housing needs, they can at least have the assurance that they have done everything possible to prepare themselves for whatever the future holds.

As people grow older these days they are presented with an endless array of products marketed with the promise of helping to make life easier for them. The advertising of these products is no longer limited to magazines and newsletters published exclusively for the geriatric set. The particular concerns of older people for their health, safety and insurance protection has caused business interests to focus on the new requirements of this growing segment of the population. This, in turn, presents a challenge of choice to a group of people who, in previous days, were not singled out for so much attention.

A highly trained physician who is new to the older person may not achieve the best results because of rushing through an appointment without allowing the patient time to talk about his or her feelings. When diagnostic tests reveal no organic problem, the discomfort may remain because the physician has not shown sufficient concern. Conversely, a person with no valid medical credentials may, from time to time, achieve a surprisingly satisfactory result simply by allowing the patient time to talk. The assurance that one has been taken seriously goes a long way toward easing the burden of unwelcome changes in life.

When change threatens the independent existence of those who have lived into old age, they may be approached by those who seek personal favors by gaining a position of friendship. Family members and established caregivers need to be alert to these intruders. Sometimes it is difficult to convince the older person that she is being set up by a flimflam artist. We are aware of instances at Holly Hall in which residents have bestowed extravagant favors upon fairly new acquaintances. Some significant losses have resulted from such schemes.

Some church people are guilty of using the elderly as a means of "doing the works of righteousness whereby they might be saved" without realizing that works alone cannot save them. Also, the life situation of those who exist in Christian community must, in its own way, minister to those who presume erroneously that they are the only ones ministering. I remember the statement of a ninety-year-old nursing care resident who exhibited the virtues of the Christian life. After being prayed over by a church visitor several times, she related to me how she was offended by the mournful nature of the prayers. She said, "I don't know how to tell this lady that she isn't helping me." Her own daily prayer, as she illustrated for me, was one of courage, faithfulness and good cheer.

All of us who work with the elderly must be careful that our prayers and our service are not offered from a mistaken idea of helpfulness. Assisting the older person as we think we would like to be assisted if our positions were reversed is not always the best rule. Unfortunately, there are not enough people who have sufficient control of their own sentiments and emotions to render a helpful and positive service to the elderly. All too frequently, we are so eager to enlist volunteers that not enough attention is given to such matters. The same situation prevails in regard to employees. Besides an evaluation of the necessary job skills there needs to be an awareness of the more subtle aspects of self-esteem, character and personal motivation. I wish that we could secure employees for work with the elderly whose style of life would not conflict severely with that of the majority of our residents. A retirement community with the objective of providing a Christian atmosphere for its residents should have employees who are committed to the Christian way of life. There are enough problems associated with caring for people who are far along in years without having people around them who are insensitive to their background of faith. An innate sense of grace, tact and understanding is important for those who are assuming volunteer tasks as well as for those who are being considered for employment.

To this point, my remarks have focused on circumstances, people and things that get in the way of healthy adjustment to change. There are, to be sure, positive attitudes to be cultivated that will make change easier to manage. While it is more difficult to make these attitudes a part of one's life if they have not been planted there in the early years, we should not accept the idea that the elderly cannot learn new things and cultivate new interests. God's enabling grace can touch some of the most unlikely candidates for change late in life. It can help them to accomplish these changes with courage, hope and even a touch of cheerfulness.

When anything possesses threatening aspects, such as a visit to a doctor or dentist, such visits can be endured far more easily when we know who will be doing the work and how it will be done. When the challenge of change is presented to those who are growing old in years, it should be handled by gaining as much knowledge as possible of whatever person, place or procedure will be new and different. This will help to ease the fear of having to deal with an issue that represents loss of control.

When a change in living arrangements becomes necessary, one of the most important things to do is to become familiar with the new place being considered. This positive approach to change gives a prospective resident of a retirement community an opportunity to become acquainted with staff and residents. It allows him or her to review the admission policies and to gain a sense of how the community views itself. Visits should be made that allow time to sample a meal, to visit the Health Center and to look over the activities schedule. Questions may need to be asked about the financial stability of the organization and the turnover rate of key personnel. This knowledge eases the anxiety associated with change and helps to prevent false expectations from causing painful adjustment experiences. Sometimes it takes a lengthy period of time to gain confidence in the decision to become part of a retirement community. It is best when such a decision is not rushed. If friends live at a certain retirement facility, it makes learning about that facility much easier.

When a man or woman moves into a retirement community, it is necessary for him or her to get used to new routines of daily living. There are new learning opportunities to be experienced as well as new outlets for creative expression to be explored. Friendships can be cultivated that will open up channels of service to the larger community.

It is a fortunate situation in new surroundings that allows for the continuation of hobbies that have been a part of one's life for many years. It is good, for example, if those who have been gardeners are able to continue working with flowers. The same thing is true for those who have enjoyed woodworking as a hobby. If a lady who has done a lot of sewing is able to have a sewing machine in her room, it can be an important factor in an acceptable adjustment to change. Many people have participated in various organizations throughout their lives. These people may find pleasure in being actively involved in a Residents' Council. Many others will enjoy bridge or dominoes.

Earnest and thoughtful prayer is an important part of the enabling process for Christian men and women as they prepare for change. The very striving of an individual for greater harmony of life is a prayerful activity. This, together with specific petitions to God for strength of spirit, will go a long way toward successfully coping with the changes of the passing years. God blesses those who give themselves up to grace in ways they are able to accept only in the rarest moments. Some of these moments may come at the time in life when they stand in the midst of the most disturbing changes.

Toward the end of life, it is good to be able to look back and observe that there were challenges along the journey that brought out an extraordinary measure of devotion, self-sacrifice or faithfulness. This exercise of remembrance involves an acknowledgement of meaning that is both reassuring for the present and instructive for future movement into a spiritual discernment of that mystery whereby "we shall not all sleep, but we shall all be changed" (1 Cor. 15:51).

Chapter 4

Preparing Each Day to Live

God asks no man whether he will accept life. That is not the choice. You must take it. The only choice is how.
—Henry Ward Beecher

I am come that they might have life, and that they might have it more abundantly.
—John 10:10, KJV

It is a pleasure to be around people who greet each day as if they are fully prepared to live. Many of the residents of Holly Hall fall into that category. They are aware of what is going on in the world and they are prepared each day to expand their knowledge. There are early morning walkers and regular participants in an exercise class. There are those who enjoy playing an early morning concert of hymns on the piano or organ. Some are interested in the weekly shopping tour and each Monday a small, devoted group may be seen leaving Holly Hall for a morning of volunteer service at a nearby hospital.

Church group meetings and Board-sponsored activities, along with the routine schedule of events, provide the residents with an interesting and entertaining selection of things to do. Musical programs, poetry appreciation and plant therapy enable life enrichment to continue as all of us grow in wisdom and in favor with each other. Everything works together to draw residents into the spirit of community living where work, rest, recreation and worship combine to make promise and fulfillment an anticipated part of growing older.

I remember a gentleman who, at the age of eighty-four, learned to make felt flowers and fly-swatter dolls. He had been an oil field worker for most of his life and he was every inch a man, but he mastered some skills that a number of women younger than he envied. On several occasions he made more money at the annual bazaar from the sale of his products than anyone else. I remember a lady beset by blindness who wrapped coat hangers and listened to great books on a record player. I think of a gentleman with arthritic knees and failing eyesight who, when asked how he was feeling, would respond, "Superfrastical!" Then there was the remarkable Miss Margaret Willits, a fine artist and musician, who played Scrabble at the age of 100 and talked about growing up on a farm in Indiana. Twenty-two of her one hundred and two years were spent at Holly Hall.

I will never forget Mrs. Mary Hunt, a lady whose good humor and charming manners were shattered by her failing eyesight and difficulty in hearing. She, with Old South courtesy, would often greet me with the words, "You're a courtly gentleman." Her grandfather, Frank Lubbock, was, as she called him, "a war governor of Texas." I found myself running after her on numerous occasions...to put batteries in her hearing aid, to get her to the Infirmary to treat a wound received from a fall just outside my office, to move her permanently to the Infirmary, which she fought against in great style ("I've got a shotgun on my lap"), and a trip to a downtown hospital late one night (I followed the blinking red light of the ambulance down almost deserted streets) and, finally, I followed her to her lot in Glenwood Cemetery one day in late November in the ninety-seventh year of her life. She loved life and she prepared each day to live in spite of adversities.

At Holly Hall there are residents who perform various volunteer chores, some official and others unofficial. They volunteer as receptionists, tour guides, flower tenders and bingo helpers. There are library assistants, commissary workers and those who enjoy visiting. Residents assist in carrying out the numerous aspects of religious life at Holly Hall. Holly Hall residents grow flowers, play bridge and go to church. They quilt, knit afghans, tat, sew, baby-sit and eat heartily.

It becomes much more difficult to face the next day when physical or mental impairments suddenly make independent living impossible. Physically handicapped residents must have assistance in getting from place to place. They must not be made to feel that it is too much trouble for someone to take them where they want to go. Those who have lost the ability to think clearly for themselves need constant orientation to their surroundings and confidence in those who are caring for them. They need to hear simple statements of information and assurance along with the reassurance that comes from a gentle touch on the hand or arm. Each employee and volunteer who comes into contact with the residents can help in some special way. It is not a complicated procedure. It involves calling the resident by name, identifying oneself and giving the reason for one's presence in the room.

The thought of having to be reliant upon others to supervise the functions of one's daily life is not at all pleasant. It is noted, however, by those who live independently, as a prospect that they may one day have to face. Residents who reach the point where such a move must be made often discover that as they receive assistance that makes life easier for them, the change is not nearly as bad as they had anticipated. We often hear the comment from those who have recently moved into the intermediate care setting, "I didn't realize that it would be so nice not having to get dressed for breakfast."

As moves are made by those who need some form of nursing assistance, we encourage friends to visit them regularly. We instruct employee care-givers in the importance of learning the unique needs and desires of each person. If the combination of our skills can prevent a cloud of depression or defeat from overcoming anyone for whom we have responsibility, we will have the satisfaction of knowing that we made a difference.

It becomes necessary, at times, for the physician to prescribe medication that will calm the depressed or confused resident. Nurses must exercise balanced judgment in reporting a condition that may lead to such prescriptions being ordered for a resident. It is a constant concern, underscored in conversations with the family, that the medication, in such instances, be kept at a minimum level. It is important also that the physician periodically examine the resident and be informed as to any changes in his or her condition.

The care of the frail elderly sometimes requires the use of restraints (vests, padded straps, geri-chairs and bedrails). Opposition to such devices has been generated by those who feel as if this procedure represents a violation of resident rights. There is no doubt that abuses of the restraint privilege occur in nursing homes. Those of us who administer care in Christ's name are particularly aware of the sensitive nature of this issue.

The nursing staff in each long-term care setting must establish care plans that consider the requirements of regulatory agencies and the individual condition of each nursing care resident. The physician is the key figure in helping to determine if restraints should be used. However, it is important that residents who must be restrained receive special attention from the nurses on each shift. Changing positions, loosening restraints and guarding against skin problems are very important duties. Sometimes restraints can be removed for short periods of time and some residents who are restrained may, at times, be assisted to their feet.

It is my opinion that the prudent use of restraints is not unwarranted. There are cases where the danger of injury dictates the use of restraints and where any other course of action, within the normal Health Care staffing pattern, would be unreasonable. Therefore, at Holly Hall, we find ourselves having to accept the fact that the only way we can provide the proper care for certain totally dependent residents is with the carefully monitored use of restraints.

When preparing each day to live is complicated by the shadow of mental confusion, there are intervention strategies that have been developed to provide assistance in getting through to those who have lost cognitive powers. They have been successful inasmuch as they enable older persons to recover important aspects of self-identity and meaning from their past. This process of guided reminiscence helps to make the day brighter for those who are all too conscious of how slowly time passes between events of other than routine importance.

Those of us who stand by the people who have reached the dependent stage of life do as much as we can in helping them to face each new day. We seek to encourage them, by our actions, to trust in the everlasting mercy of the God who holds tomorrow. This trust, however, must be evidenced daily on behalf of those who rely on caring hands. It comes through the self-giving that validates our calling. It speaks of taking the time we have been given and offering it back to God in service that affirms the lives of those who have lived longest upon the earth. Our reward is an abundant harvest of love that God, in Christ, has made available through the hands that are extended to us in offering and in supplication.

Jesus said, as recorded in John's Gospel, that abundant life was an objective of his dwelling among us. While there is more to the life of which Jesus spoke than many of us may realize, abundant life, commonly understood, is illusory to those who wonder why God is letting them live so long. Men and women must start early, before retirement age, to cultivate the vision of a fulfilled life. Bitterness can take over a life that has no sense of direction. A strong spiritual dimension enables people of all ages to live as if God cares and as if there are routines of daily devotion and friendship to be celebrated.

Those who prepare to live each day in the abundance of God's love and grace must meet the challenge of accepting those for whom life seems to have lost all meaning and purpose. They need to be cross-bearers for the spiritually defeated who manifest their weakness by seeking to magnify the weaknesses they perceive in others, in the place where they live and in the world that God has made. This cross-bearing activity is part of the call to Christian discipleship. It is an imperative of the evangel. Preparing each day to live includes helping others to do the same. It involves letting the light shine in the places where darkness has the best chance to be victorious. It means being instructed daily by "the way, the truth and the life."

Chapter 5

When Tempests Rage About

You must live with people to know their problems, and live with God in order to solve them.
—P. T. Forsyth

At Holly Hall, where anywhere from 150 to 175 people aged 65 and over live together, there are many trials and tribulations. There are conflicts of personality; there are real and imagined abuses of privilege; there is loneliness and sorrow, fierce independence of thought and action, and the most possessive dependencies. There are many physical problems and an abundance of aggravating annoyances that beg for the wisdom of Solomon to resolve them. So many of the tempests occur as the result of a combination of frustrating inactivity, loss of physical vitality, reduction of mental alertness, uncertainty over the future and some legitimate grievances over the apparent injustices that some residents must endure.

Requirements of the Task

Living with the elderly involves accepting them as adults and taking each conversation, each communication of a need and each request for advice with complete seriousness. Solutions to problems do vary, however, according to the situation and the people involved. While I may advise one person to take the initiative in settling a grievance with another, in another instance I may bring both parties into my office for a more direct approach to solving whatever the problem may be. I may offer one person a way to solve a problem, whereas I may decline to offer any solution to another person with the same problem.

My knowledge of the residents and their backgrounds is such that I feel some of the problems they report to me will solve themselves. Listening and showing concern is of primary importance in these cases. Quite often, the residents will know before they come in that there is nothing that can be done. They just want to know that they will be listened to seriously. They want someone to show interest in them and to be aware of what they have on their minds.

Sadly, many problems are those which are imagined or exaggerated to the point of absurdity. However, it should be understood that most of the time an imagined problem also requires some kind of solution. It should not be allowed to go unanswered. For example, a resident who is sure that someone is up on the roof at night trying to get into her room really has a much more difficult problem to solve than one whose bathroom has developed a leaky faucet. While each person must be received as an adult and treated with respect, the problems presented by each person must be dealt with according to knowledge of that person's individual condition and need. If a resident reports that she has been forced into moving into a nursing care room against her will, and I know that she can neither remember the reason why such a move has had to be made nor appreciate it in any way, I do not agree with her (with the rationalization that an explanation of the move will make no difference since she cannot remember anyway). Neither do I dismiss her with the implication that I am too busy to explain.

I try to reason with her, sometimes over and over, about the advantage of her new location. I take a strong, positive approach and emphasize the greater safety and added convenience of her new room.

There are times when the general rule of complete honesty is suspended in favor of what amounts to a therapy of "joining the fantasy." The treatment of people with the problem of imagining all manner of bizarre happenings is done with greater success, at times, by involving oneself in the story as if it were true. Trying to argue the person into accepting the fact that such things are not going on often provokes anger and distrust.

When I came to Holly Hall, a lady in the Infirmary was suffering from what seemed to be a severe persecution complex. She imagined that someone was seeking to have her murdered and that "he" had cohorts inside of the building who were involved in the detailed plan to carry it out. Each day there was some new twist to the same nightmarish story that revolved around this lady's fearful idea that she was about to be killed. Nothing we did to comfort her was successful—perhaps because we were trying to make her believe that it was not true. Some of those around her, I'm sure, told her that she was not making any sense or was out of her mind. One notable exception was a very alert Board member who one day, in a beautifully spontaneous response, countered her tale of woe with the quick reply, "The plans have been changed." This gave me the clue I needed to follow a new track. I would not argue that her wild tale was just not true, nor would I utter words of comfort that did not ease her mind at all. But, through a variety of tactical maneuvers, I sought to thwart the plan of the would-be assassin. When she would talk about the number of people "he" had on the "inside," I would assert that the number working for me far exceeded those who were in "his" gang and that they would be able to prevent the plan from being carried out. If the feared mastermind behind the plot was located on a high tower outside (as she described it one day), keeping watch for just the right time to commit the crime, I would tell her that I had outside sentries watching his every move. If she told me that "they" stayed up late, I would tell her that my people never slept. Along with the persistence of my strategic moves to counter every new version of the same drastic theme, I started having this lady repeat, in some form, a statement of trust in God each evening as I visited her room. While I cannot to this day be sure what fortunate combination of treatment measures was responsible for the change, I do know that her fears gradually subsided and that she spent her remaining years at Holly Hall in a relatively calm state of mind.

If an Infirmary resident who is known to be disoriented reports that she has been mistreated, it should not be assumed that she imagined it. Although it is extremely difficult to ascertain the reliability of such reports, a thorough effort is made to find out what, if anything, happened.

One who always is complaining should not be avoided because of her litany of grievances. This person has a need, even if it must be discovered beneath the words that have been spoken. Although I do not always answer complaints that have no basis in fact with the assurance that something will be done, I do try to treat the actual problem that seems to have given rise to such complaints.

Many tempests are generated by the perpetual "grapevine" rumors that grow and are cultivated to the extent that the anxiety level of certain individuals is heightened considerably. Sometimes, just coming by the office to get the facts straight is sufficient. This is encouraged. At other times it takes more patient listening and reassurance to ease the troubled mind. Sometimes a problem requires assistance from the resident's family. Sometimes it is a family member who calls our attention to the problem. Some problems are only eased, not solved. In every instance I acknowledge God's partnership in the counseling process, but I must admit that there are some tempests that, in cowardice or wisdom, I leave to God alone to tame.

One of the most troubling shadows of despair that grips many of our people in uncertainty over what may happen to them in the future. Most of the residents chose to live at Holly Hall in order to help solve that uneasy feeling. They acknowledge that, although they don't know *what* will happen to them, they will at least know *where* it will happen. However, in being able to observe the affects of aging on others they may, in some instances, become more anxious over what, where and when something undesirable will happen to them. They begin to fear a stroke or a fractured hip. They dread the prospect of having to be moved to one of the nursing care areas. They sign statements to be given to their doctor, family and others specifying that they do not want their lives prolonged by artificial or heroic measures if they reach the point where the chance for meaningful recovery is gone. Sometimes their anxiety is over the illness of a loved one or a problem in the family.

When a man determines that his productive years are over, that all the happy and personally fulfilling times are in his past, it is all too easy to sit down in dejection and imagine how it would be best for life to end. In a spiritual sense death already may have claimed him. Maybe the men and women who feel this way are the ones who gave up too quickly during their earlier years when confronted with some difficult situation. There are people in every age group who tend to resign themselves to failure when they are presented with what they consider to be an insurmountable obstacle. The lesson of *The Little Engine that Could* is as appropriate for old age as it is for childhood. A similar message seems to echo from the poem of Dylan Thomas, "Do Not Go Gentle into that Good Night." [1] The words seem to be a call to resist passage into death until the last breath:

Old age must burn and rave at close of day;
Rage, rage against the dying of the light.

I applaud that same spirit in every effective blow raised against the decaying effects of idleness. Exercise of mind and body for as long as possible is essential to wholesomeness of life. Limbs that are not used will soon grow useless and flabby. Minds that are not engaged in pleasant and constructive thoughts will be more apt to be filled with despair and pessimism or they will much more quickly reach the point where recall is limited to bits and pieces from years long gone. This kind of gloom was expressed in passages from Proust's *Remembrance of Things Past.*

My deepest regret is that I do not always see those who, on a given day, may need me the most. They may not be able to get to my office or they may be hesitant about getting word to me. They may decide that it is too trivial. I try, for every resident, to be the person who has plenty of time. It is a mistake for anyone working with older people to rush them away or to ignore their need for conversation. There are times, of course, when it is necessary to apologize for not having time at the moment, but a conference should not be delayed except for the most important reasons. I do not believe in making reference to being busy or overworked. I respect the person who does not complain about long hours but who will, nonetheless, take time for personal and family recreation.

Making Conversation Count

In working with the elderly I try to be a good listener. This means hearing what is said with that delicate inner ear that can determine the real need of the person, whether or not it is clearly expressed. Quite often the words that are spoken in response to an individual's needs are words of encouragement and hope. Here, of course, great care should be exercised. Traditional words of comfort and assurance may not be adequate for some people. There must be more than a surface knowledge of the person to whom counsel is being offered. Sometimes it is very appropriate to quote Scripture. I find myself using the words attributed to Jesus, especially, "In this world you will have tribulation; but be of good cheer, for I have overcome the world," and, "I will not leave you comfortless." On some occasions the words of familiar hymns come to mind. One day I just started saying the words, "Be not dismayed what'ere betide, God will take care of you. Beneath His wings of love abide, God will take care of you." When I had finished, the dear lady, obviously comforted, said, "My mother used to say the words of that hymn each night as she tucked me into bed." I had struck a responsive chord.

Sometimes bits of poetry will come to mind that serve a special purpose of identification. One day as I walked past the open door of a room in the Infirmary a high, cracked voice called my name. I walked back to the small, stroke-diminished frame of one who, in her more active days at Holly Hall, had raged over her then restricted activity. She said, "I'm trying to remember the words of a poem. I can't find anyone who knows it." By coincidence it was Leigh Hunt's "Abou Ben Adhem," which I had memorized quite a long time ago. I started, hesitantly at first, to repeat the lines. Her eyes brightened and she joined me as best she could. We got through the poem together and she said, "Thank you so much, I thought when I saw you that if anyone knew 'Abou Ben Adhem', you would. I learned it in school many years ago and I've been trying so hard to remember it."

Sometimes I pray with a resident after a visit and sometimes I do not. Sometimes I extend a simple "God bless you" to them or a benediction. In the way God has of using us for special purposes, there are clues for our words and deeds, given to us by God, if we have cultivated a spiritual sensitivity to the needs of others. Quite often the clue will be provided by the resident. However, no one can get the message right every time. I may read the sign incorrectly or fail to detect a change in a certain pattern of behavior that signals the necessity of a different response.

Encouraging older persons to accept the circumstances in which they find themselves is not always desirable. It may be interpreted as advising them to give up trying to make things work right. Nor should we be angry or remorseful if our best advice goes unheeded. In fact, we should be careful about coming out with specific recommendations for their lives. Counseling with the elderly must, of necessity, be a process. It should tend toward encouragement while opening the possibility for an adjustment in thought that will, perhaps, lead to an independent decision to accept less responsibility or to accept a move to another location. Our design must not be so much to tell the older person what to do or think as it is to plant some thoughts that may enable him to reach the decision on his own. It is upsetting to everyone when that strategy is not successful. In those instances we are often faced with the task of having to make very direct statements to that person regarding a change that must be made. There are times when the situation requires us to tell the resident about the necessity of a move that they are strongly resisting and then see to it that the move is accomplished.

We must accept the frustrating task, in counseling the elderly, of having to start the process over and over. Forgetfulness, uncertainty and an excessive dependency will bring certain residents back many times, thereby presenting us with the necessity of saying the same thing to the same person over and over. But we must remember that if they did not trust who we are and what we are saying, they would have one less cause for being satisfied with where they are. Also, we have to keep before us the realization that as people grow older the possibilities increase for them not to be able to deal with the routine of daily living on an acceptably rational level. At times we may find ourselves giving reassurance in response to completely irrelevant concerns. This requires imagination and insight as well as a keen sense of humor and the ability to handle real and imagined problems with equal seriousness. There must be optimism tempered with a realistic understanding of what may happen in old age that is unique for each person. This situation asks for people of emotional maturity in helping positions; people who have confidence in themselves without taking themselves too seriously. Friendships should not be cultivated in these relationships to the extent that freedom to serve the real needs of the person is jeopardized. This applies to families of residents as well. This is not to say that we should not think of them as friends. But if we have favorites it should never be obvious. Kindness and consideration should be extended to everyone on an equal basis and even the most unlovable in our sphere of responsibility should know that we can be counted on to assist them without the slightest hesitation.

We must be prepared, in relating to people of advanced years, to offer our best in every need that presents itself. There should be time for study and continuing education in order to keep up with the latest information in the field of gerontology. When tempests rage about the heads of those who are moving through the last years of their earthly pilgrimage, there must be special people to whom they can go, trusted confidants, who will know how to listen and what to do and say. These individuals may serve as pastor and priest in a way that a resident's own minister cannot or will not. There are occasions when it is necessary to counsel with family members concerning their feelings about the aging process in general or a father or mother in particular.

Finally

In my work at Holly Hall, I am called upon to interpret Board decisions and employee attitudes. I must set the example for good relations between residents and employees and obtain the best departmental cooperation possible in order to make resident care the foremost consideration of employment. I have threaded needles and assisted in preparing wills. I perform minor repairs on eye-glasses and review insurance policies. Sometimes, in emergency situations, I have handled a mop. I lean to the side of softness and leniency in dealing with personal idiosyncrasies so long as the spirit of community is not violated.

It might be asked how one can have a sense of fulfillment within the complexities of a ministry that is subject to so many suggestions as to how it could be done better. It comes only as one is fully aware that one does not have the right answer to every question or the best solution to every personal crisis. On the other hand, it exists only as one does not give way to self-pity or defensiveness. Mistakes must be admitted. Complete responsibility must be assumed. Every effort must be made to correct problems and find the right answers. Flexibility is important. A desire to make life more pleasant and pain more bearable is necessary. This is a part of the challenge I face every day. But I do not do it without the assistance of a competent and dedicated staff who have learned how to be kind and, at times, necessarily firm in carrying out their assignments. What is equally important is the strong support I receive from the Board of Directors and an involved family that includes a wife who is a Holly Hall volunteer and who assists me in ways too numerous to name.

Chapter 6

Receiving the Gifts

The Christmas story...is not about how blessed it is to be givers, but how essential it is to see ourselves as receivers.
—William H. Willimon

People who regularly come in contact with the residents of Holly Hall often find themselves being offered gifts by the residents. While some occasions demand that a gift be turned down, it is, for the most part, important to accept the gift as a symbol of our acceptance of the giver. While it is possible that a gift may be offered with the expectation of getting something in return, I find that the older people within my circle of concern are beautifully spontaneous givers whose giving provides an important feeling of self-worth. It is, perhaps unconsciously, a sign of independence and freedom to be able to give something away. It establishes the giver as one who has something to offer another as a token of appreciation for being kind and helpful.

From the beginning of our time of service at Holly Hall, we have received a variety of gifts from the residents, ranging from items of food (sometimes cooked by them) to poems (sometimes composed by them). When our children were young they were singled out to be the recipients of countless gifts. The widow of a ship's captain gave them a soft music box and a festive clown doll. She happened to be a lady who had not been blessed with children of her own and, as one with limited income, her gifts might have represented, to anyone of thrifty persuasion, an unnecessary extravagance.

There were gifts of candy at Halloween and an outpouring of Christmas gifts. We have received, as a family, quite a few decorations that we place on or under the Christmas tree during Advent, each one reminding us of the resident who made it. There was, one Christmas, a set of figurines representing those who were a part of the scriptural drama of the birth of Jesus. There have been styrofoam angels and, once, a carefully crafted oblong frame holding a small photograph of me (I still do not know how the resident obtained the photo). We have been given, at various times, knitted slippers, afghans, plates, wrapped coat-hangers, candles, plants, note paper, a ceramic quail and an old coin. We have been given books, baskets of fruit, bouquets of flowers and boxes of candy. One of the most touching gifts from the residents of Holly Hall came about upon the death of my mother. She was living at Happy Harbor, a non-profit intermediate care facility. Our residents gave memorial gifts to that Home in a generous act of respect and sympathy. Receiving the abundance of gifts, as we have, has given us an unusual opportunity to learn how to be receivers without, at any time, expecting anything of those whom we have been called to serve. All of these gifts mark us as those who have, in a sense, found favor in the eyes of those with whom we share certain experiences of living.

As those who feel close to us, in the sense of trust and familial belonging, the residents of Holly Hall open their lives to us in interesting ways. In listening to their stories, we are allowing them to establish their identity with us and at the same time our knowledge is broadened and our lives enriched. People who have reached an advanced age do not share their memories with just anyone (aches and pains maybe, but not memories). Even so, we hear only what they choose to share and we do not hear from everyone. As the years pass, we add to the storehouse of our memories the fresh stories new residents tell of events in time that, because of a special meaning to them, have become a part of who they are.

We are taught, sometimes in the most unstructured ways, by the residents of this community. We are given genuine pearls of wisdom. Many of our residents have made outstanding contributions to the common good as teachers and as church and community leaders. Some of them continue to make these contributions. There are examples among our residents of achievement in literature, art and music. Others have made their mark in business and labor and through the valuable gifts of parenting and household management. What they are able to teach us about life can be thought of as the intangible gifts.

We also receive from our residents a look forward to what life might be like later on for those of us who are younger. From those who possess spiritual insight, we are able to glimpse the future in a way that allows us to claim "winter grace" as a part of our present being and doing. It is a kind of "getting ready" that does not mean following a precise advance planning schedule. Instead, it is being aware, each day, of a dimension of existence that comes from beyond our earth-bound sensitivities. It is the means whereby prophecy is able to point us to the dawning of a new age, soul-refreshing music is able to draw us heavenward and the drama of the liturgy is able to make us particularly conscious of what God has done for us in Christ. As the words of the familiar hymn by Ernest Shurtleff express it, "Through days of preparation, Thy grace has made us strong." This is the gift of those who have lived long in faithfulness to the Gospel. We are thankful for those by whom we are still being instructed. "Part of [that] host has crossed the flood and part are crossing now." (Charles Wesley)

Many people are affected by the generosity of our family of residents at Holly Hall. It is important to note that they are also generous to each other. There are those who take gifts of fruit or cookies to nursing care residents. Some of the more able residents read to those with poor eyesight and assist, in special ways, those who are not feeling well. They offer words of encouragement to those who spend long hours in waiting for the next meal, the next bath or the next celebration of the Sacrament of Holy Communion.

One very interesting lady who made her home at Holly Hall for a number of years left little notes on my desk from time to time containing clever verses or sayings that she had gathered from a variety of sources. The writing of one of her sources was signed "Cheerful Cherub." After awhile, anything she left that she had written was signed "Cheerful Cherub #2." When she would see me in the hall, often before the noon meal, she would look at me as if to say, "What did you think about that one?" She was a pioneer, and what she gave Holly Hall would open the door to a startling change in the "understood" dress code of the community.

Up to the early years of the 70s, there had been no bending of the established custom that the ladies of Holly Hall did not wear "men's clothing" (slacks or pant suits). I did not have occasion to question that practice until M. B. (somewhat on the heavy side) asked me one day what I would do if she wore slacks to dinner. I wasn't sure how to answer that question, so I did what I had learned was the best approach to proposals that could have undesirable repercussions if they were carried out...I stalled for time. However, she was persistent. She presented some very logical reasons to me for allowing the change to occur. She said, "Look at me. I'm big—I need some way to cover up these legs!" She had a good sense of humor, an attractive smile and a roving eye. (Our Cheerful Cherub once latched onto a man visiting Holly Hall who happened to ask her where he could get a cup of coffee. Her response to that question was "Come with me, honey." When some ladies looked in on them, having coffee together in the Employee's Dining Room, she called out, "Buzz off girls, this one's mine.") I finally said to her, "All right, I'll allow you to wear the slacks, but you must be prepared for the criticism you will receive." I was, of course, thinking about the criticism that I might receive as well.

I will never forget the moment when she stepped out of her room on "Fifth Avenue," as Corridor Five was called in those days. I was looking toward her room from Corridor One when she appeared. She bowed slightly at the waist and then lifted her head. Her chin was slightly elevated. Her bearing conveyed an obvious command to me. "Move out of the way, Mister Administrator, I'm coming through." She was bold enough to make it work. There was some criticism, but she (and I) absorbed it quite well. The Holly Hall residents today, who enjoy the convenience of dressing more comfortably as they choose, owe this freedom, at least in part, to Cheerful Cherub #2 who, some years later, couldn't understand why I wanted her to live when she was ready, cheerfully, to die.

One aspect of receiving gifts that should be mentioned relates to a need we all have to cultivate a graceful awareness of how to be receivers. Some of the residents of Holly Hall have been exemplary givers but, like many people of every age and station in life, have not been as good at receiving gifts. There are residents who feel guilty over having part of their care subsidized by Holly Hall. It is difficult to keep some of those with modest financial resources from feeling like second class residents. They grew up learning the importance of paying bills on time and in the full amount. They find it hard to be receivers. There are a few, on the other hand, who are sadly deficient in receiving gifts because they take the gift (and the giver) for granted. This is a sad commentary on the influences that have shaped their lives.

Unfortunately, there are people at every economic and social level who use every opportunity to get what they want. When they are offered a gift it is never the right color or the right size. If the gift is monetary, it is never enough. Organizations and philanthropic individuals who share their resources out of a generous concern for human need discover, to their disappointment, that some upon whom their gifts are bestowed are unable or unwilling to respond appreciatively. Fortunately, most of those to whom we offer the gift of caring service at Holly Hall are truly grateful for what they receive and let us know it in unusual and endearing ways. Those who are privately held in the highest esteem are those at every level of financial ability who do not in any obvious way connect what they receive to what they pay. They are the ones who appear to have, in their own way, inherited the earth.

I realize the importance to all of us of receiving new gifts, special surprises, even as we should not take for granted the routine gifts of each day or the gifts of those once-a-year days that validate the love others have for us. Many gifts leave us not knowing exactly how to respond. Our words of thanks do not always deliver the feeling that we have inside. So we immediately start thinking about what we can get or do for that friend or loved one that will say thanks in a way that we cannot accomplish with words. We are not very good at receiving gifts. Maybe it is because we have not learned to live according to the meaning of unconditional love (as givers and receivers).

The gift of love, often symbolized by tangible gifts, is a great blessing to receive. It is revealed through faith by the gift of Christ, the Son of God, to the world. "For God so loved the world, that he gave his only begotten Son..." (John 3:16) Sadly, we know how the powers of the world received Him. But to those who receive Him, as heirs of the promise, there is the fulfillment of joy. "He awakens within us," wrote Paul Tournier, "an altogether new concern for it [the world]. Then, just as little children, we can enjoy all the little gifts of this earthly life, seeing in them so many signs of that great and final gift which awaits us." [2]

Part II

Beginning, for the most part, with Chapter 7, "The Losses of Old Age—Magnified and Overcome," there may be noted a slight shift in the style and purpose of my writing. This can be attributed to the personally liberating experience associated with the preparatory phase of the Doctor of Ministry studies at St. Paul School of Theology and the application of that entire program to life at Holly Hall. These chapters seek to elevate to a salutary dimension those aspects of aging that are commonly viewed as negative. They relate to spiritual awareness and friendships for life during the period of loss and decline that we tend, perhaps too much, to associate with growing old. They continue to reflect the answers grace provides to the questions that challenge Christian commitment during the years that, for many people, call for redefining the meaning of life.

Chapter 7

The Losses of Old Age—Magnified and Overcome

Since grief but aggravates thy loss,
Grieve not for what is past.
—Anonymous

For many, all of life has been focused upon gaining things as well as enjoying the intangible rewards of acceptance, place and security. Then, sometimes with alarming swiftness, there begins a time when loss is the by-word of existence. This is, without doubt, a most disturbing change. Production ceases or is greatly reduced. Adult children go away with children of their own who require their quality hours. Friends of many years begin, one by one, to die or move to other places. Possessions diminish and, in time, require management by others. In addition, there are losses of hearing, sight, mental and physical dexterity, hair, sexual virility, the more subtle losses of influence and, at last, respect. To be told that one is "losing it" earlier in life may be nothing more than a desire, on the part of another person, to inflict psychological pain, but to experience first hand the specific losses of old age is a challenge of great magnitude to the human spirit. Redefining values in order to help cope with the losses of old age is very important. It is prompted as we examine in more detail the phenomenon of loss/diminishment/decline whereby we may all too easily view the last years of life in a predominantly negative light.

There are many examples in literature that depict the losses we may expect if we live long enough. In Shakespeare's play, *As You Like It*, we read the following lines:

Last scene of all, That ends this strange, eventful history, Is second childishness, and mere oblivion, Sans teeth, sans eyes, sans taste, sans everything.

Modern advertising provides no relief from that same theme. Older people are used, almost exclusively, to promote products that are supposed to ease the burden or pain of certain losses, e.g., something to mitigate the loss of a good digestive system, healthy skin, regularity or teeth. Add to what already has been mentioned the loss of home, automobile and, later, the ability to sign checks, and it is easily predictable that the "loss syndrome" will, except in very unusual circumstances, consume the older person.

In thinking about the weight of some of the earliest influences of life, we realize that there are people whose entire history is interwoven with a tragic sense of loss. Men and women may have endured, as children, various kinds of deprivation. Perhaps, as infants, some of our older acquaintances did not receive a full measure of love and caring nurture from their parents. Then, later on, they developed a feeling of being left out, of being taken advantage of by others and of losing their hold upon the things of value they did possess. When old age brings other losses to this type of person he becomes even more mentally impoverished. Sometimes he becomes bitter over what he feels God has done to him. Never having possessed adequate self-worth, he proceeds to lose what little he has and before long becomes resigned to the ultimate loss—that of life itself.

Is it any wonder, then, that many older people are obsessed with the idea of loss and tend to imagine losses even when there have been none? Caregivers in retirement communities and nursing homes are painfully aware of the familiar cry, "It is gone! They have taken my watch, my robe, my jewelry, my candy, my money." It seems as if each day brings a new story of something valuable that has disappeared from the room of one of the residents.

One of the greatest challenges to maintaining a calm expression and self-control is when the accusing finger is pointed at the administrator, staff and everyone in sight over what is imagined to be a conspiracy of theft. The individual is convinced that the valuable item has been taken, not just lost in the room, misplaced, or in the hands of a family member. The unfortunate truth that there are thefts from time to time (confounding us by the apparent disregard some people have for the rights of the elderly) makes the suggestion of another possibility implausible and almost always subject to bitter rejection. The idea of anything other than deliberate pilferage is seldom entertained. Confession of the possibility of forgetting what was done with the item or items would be admitting to the loss of mental acuity.

The ways in which possessions disappear from a room are unlimited. A lady went into the room of another resident who had left her door unlocked and removed a dress. The "theft" was reported. Much later it was revealed that the dress was on loan. The one who had loaned the dress couldn't convince her friend that she had not given her the dress. Therefore, she took the matter into her own hands to recover her property. Another lady kept reporting losses of money. Several years later, following her death, as her family was cleaning out her room, they happened to notice the edge of a five-dollar bill sticking out from the back of a picture frame. Upon examining other pictures, over eighty dollars was discovered. We had never been able to satisfy her demand that we catch the thief who was making off with her money.

Items are given to family members and the instances of such giving are forgotten. Family members take things out of the room with the thought that "Mother will not need this any longer." Later, "Mother" reports them to be stolen. Residents give things away, forget all about it, and report them stolen. Even though we realize that circumstances such as these are part of what we must accept, there are times when we grow weary of such consuming passions.

"It's terrible," shouts an irate daughter of a resident in the Health Center, "that Mother cannot keep anything of value in her room!" "Quite so," I reply, "but you must realize that she is no longer able to appreciate having such items with her." "That's beside the point," she says in return. "They are a part of her life and I want to see them in her room whenever I come for a visit." I understand the daughter's lament, but it is obvious that she does not want to accept the fact that her mother has lost something more valuable than her hand-painted bud vase and that, in trying to keep things as "they always have been," she is fighting against what she perceives are her own impending loss.

What can be done about accepting the inevitable losses of life that come as one grows older? What can we say to those whose bodily mechanisms seem to topple like a row of dominos when one loss button is pushed? What consolation can we offer to the cry, "It is gone"? How can we keep our heads on straight in the midst of conflicts arising from the sadness and anger of aging's down side? What could Browning possibly have meant when he wrote the words, concerning growing old, "the best is yet to be"?

Much of what can be said in response to these questions is by way of repeated emphasis on how important the earliest influences of life are in determining what we shall be and do. A shortage of love, for example, often leads to an excess of lust for power and possessions. It is an unfortunate circumstance that those in their later years who lack the insight of spiritual wisdom are not likely to understand the blessing of self-emptying wherein, by grace, their cup may overflow. Frenetically pursuing the goals of business and personal achievement limits the possibility of fulfilling existence in Christ. But, in the ripe December years, a greater awareness of God's gifts may quietly invade the senses, helping to cover the inevitable losses. This is depicted in William Butler Year's "Sailing to Byzantium":

An aged man is but a paltry thing,
A tattered coat upon a stick, unless
Soul clap its hands and sing, and louder sing
For every tatter in its mortal dress.[3]

In the soul-celebrating rhythms of returning and rest old age rehearses the songs of Zion. Meanwhile, bright memories and trusted friends help to make living through losses more bearable. In Shakespeare's Sonnet No. 30 we discover these words of assurance:

But if the while I think on thee, dear friend, All losses are restor'd and sorrows end.

In addition to the bonding rituals of faith and the firm reliance upon cultivated spiritual assets to help ease the sorrow of losing various sorts of "valuable cargo," there is the need, at last, for acquiescence. To say "yes" to life means saying "yes" to all of it. When apparent reversals begin to cut into independence and self-management, hopefully there will be available a friend, confidant or, simply, some honest helper (remember "The Death of Ivan Ilyich") to speak the blessed truth. To come to terms with our humanity is, in some way, to invoke the same servant voice that Philip of Macedon did with the one whose duty it was to wake him each morning with the words, "Remember, Philip, thou too must die." The sting of that constant reminder is swallowed up in the triumphant hope of the resurrection which offers us, now and at last, the peace of Christ.

So, "the best is yet to be," as we grow older, in the same sense that we call the day Jesus died on the cross "Good Friday." It is best as a time of summing up, of being still and completing the journey that draws us toward "dying in the Lord" whose ultimately protective grasp has held us while we have lived through "many dangers, toils and snares." We are moving toward "a further union, a deeper communion," as T.S. Eliot wrote in "Four Quartets." The truth of living and dying in the faith may be expressed as it was at the beginning of Chapter 1, "In my end is my beginning."

Chapter 8

Toward a Greater Spiritual Awareness

Finally, all of you, have unity of spirit, sympathy, love of [one another], a tender heart and a humble mind.
—1 Peter 3:8

Holly Hall has never been without a strong influence of church life. It was brought into existence by the combined organizational planning of church people representing several Christian denominations. There always has been a distinct Christian purpose underlying the efforts to raise money, recruit volunteers and admit residents. Even before the Chapel was built in 1958, regular worship services were held in the main dining room. Church meetings at Holly Hall, with residents as guests, have been a traditional activity for many years. It would be natural, then, to ask how there could be a need for greater spiritual awareness in the lives of the residents.

I felt, from the first years of my employment at Holly Hall, the need for a greater sense of Christian community. It related to what I perceived was a failure to be more direct in purpose as a distinct segment of the Body of Christ. Individuals representing different denominations were meeting in one place, but seemed as though they were engaged in personal devotions. Although my training in Christian worship caused me to realize what we were not accomplishing in our services together, I did not have the motivation or adequate understanding to put something new and untested into the minds of the residents for consideration. I saw the great opportunity we had for ministry to each other if we could only draw strength from our common commitment to the saving grace of Jesus Christ.

I arrived at last, through the blessing of doctoral studies, at a design for Christian ministry with the residents of Holly Hall. After consultation with some of the residents, it was decided to call our new venture "Christian Life Emphasis." It was to involve the residents in the process of Christian guidance, first through rituals that would affirm the individual as an important part of the community of faith.

A crucial factor in the organization of the first Christian Life Emphasis Council was the appointment of a Chairperson who possessed strong leadership qualities as well as a history of devoted Christian service. I chose Mrs. Annanelle Curran, a member of Bering Memorial United Methodist Church. Preliminary conversations with her set the stage for what we knew, in faith, we should be doing at Holly Hall. Naming members to serve on the first Council was not difficult. We selected those who were engaged in doing things that were related to Christian life and worship at the time, namely, the one who taught the Bible Study Class, the one who scheduled ministers for chapel services, the one who kept the calendar for meal blessings, an organist, communion assistants, one who was interested in service projects and a cottage resident. Including the Assistant Administrator and myself, there were eleven present for the first Council meeting.

Many ideas were discussed at that first meeting. We talked about having a room blessing each time we welcomed a new resident into Holly Hall. It was then mentioned that we ought to do something to mark the end of each new resident's three-month probation. It was recommended that we distribute a lectionary for residents to follow through the year so that everyone would be reading the same Scripture lesson each day. A proposed "Commitment to Christian Life Emphasis" was presented and accepted. Council members divided up the corridors for the purpose of explaining Christian Life Emphasis (CLE) to the other residents and to give out the commitment form and the lectionary. Prior to the visits, signs had been posted on the bulletin boards—"Look For CLE!"—which aroused curiosity. I reported what was happening to the Board of Directors. It was an exciting time!

The Room Blessing has proved to be a meaningful way to define our Christian intent to each new resident. Our entry, as friends, into the room is a welcoming ceremony. It has a close kinship with baptism as a sacramental initiation into the community. It signifies entry into a uniquely Christian way of living together. In a sense, the blessing includes all of the things that the resident has packed up and brought with her (including the storehouse of memories that accompany possessions into the new place).

Our service to mark the end of probation (three months) affords us the opportunity to confirm the position of each new resident as a fully accepted member of the Holly Hall community. Rites of confirmation and initiation have been a part of

Christian worship for centuries. While not all of our residents come from church traditions that have confirmation services, they all seem to understand and appreciate the ritual acknowledgement of their acceptance. It is confirming evidence in Christian ceremony that they are, once again, settled. As I look into their faces, witness hugs and hear exclamations of joy, I see possibilities for a new dynamic of belonging in which re-formation of life, in the Christian sense, may mark the existence of those who become residents. As friendships are made for the rest of the journey, the context in which they are nurtured can be attributed to the providence of God. This providence, Albert Outler has told us, "means the provision of a community of faith and grace in which men [and women] may cultivate their consciousness of God's presence and imperative love, in Word and Sacrament, in faithful witness and sacrificial service."[4] (Rituals of Belonging are found in Appendix A.)

Every activity of a religious nature comes under the general oversight of the CLE Council. Special services of worship are planned and outreach projects are carried out. Unique times of "upholding" emerge spontaneously.

Celebration of the Sacrament of the Lord's Supper for Holly Hall residents who receive routine nursing care is a highly significant worship experience once a month. It represents a notable departure from the previous way nursing care residents received communion. For years, I accepted the practice of having the guest minister at our chapel communion service distribute the elements immediately following the service in the chapel. A few of the residents gathered in the Infirmary solarium and many others remained in their rooms. It was a long process and was keyed more to the individual resident than to any sense of corporate worship. It left the impression that these people were being denied the full privilege of the Lord's Table. Now, almost all of the residents are brought out to the service. They gather, many in wheelchairs, in the solarium and out into the adjoining hallway. The kitchen is located just across from the Table, which is covered with a white cloth and centered with a cross and stand for the Bible. After a greeting, familiar hymns are sung and we participate in the "passing of the peace" as the resident pianist plays "Blest Be the Tie That Binds Our Hearts in Christian Love." As the "peace" concludes, I go into an adjacent office where I put on a robe and stole (signifying my role as celebrant). As I move back to the Table, we recite together the Lord's prayer or the Twenty-Third Psalm. Then I call for the offering of the gifts of God. The first gift is the Holy Bible, carried by the Assistant Administrator. This is followed by Dietary personnel bearing the paten (which holds the loaf of bread that has been baked in the Holly Hall kitchen) and the chalice. These are placed on the Table. The reading of the Gospel Lesson is followed by the Prayer of Thanksgiving. The bread is broken and the chalice is uplifted. The elements are, by intinction, placed into the mouth of each resident in attendance.

The Nursing Care Communion holds a powerful meaning for those who cannot care for themselves as, in the process of eucharistic celebration, they are affirmed in the depths of their being. Appendix B contains notes on Nursing Care Communion.

A "Passage" within Holly Hall, requiring prayerful support and upholding, is associated with a move from an area where total independence is required to an area where necessary nursing assistance is provided. A special time of recognition and encouragement speaks to staff and to other residents of our concern for the need of each resident for the embrace of Christian love.

Sometimes the idea of having to give up a degree of independence in a move to more confined quarters is more difficult for family members to understand than it is for the resident. A challenge is presented to us as we seek to counteract the anxiety that such a move often produces.

"Affirmation of Life" was accepted by the CLE Council as the perspective in which the community will acknowledge the death of a resident. The final "Passage" is observed through different kinds of services but always at Holly Hall in such a way that will underscore the spirit of belonging that has become such a vital part of the CLE ministry.

In addition to the regularly scheduled services and activities, there are numerous acts of caring for each other among the residents that go largely unnoticed. There are times of Bible reading and prayer in the rooms, visits by those who live independently to those who regularly need nursing assistance and special times of listening, sharing a gift of something to eat, touching the hand of another or simply being with them. Many incidents point to an obvious link with the Christian Life Emphasis movement at Holly Hall. I have included a description of some of these incidents in Appendix C.

The challenge we face is to stimulate engagement in the rituals of our life together that will quietly supplant those associated with church activities which, too often, are structured in such a manner that older members are discouraged from participation. We also seek to direct the spiritual life of our residents toward the celebration of being itself.

The majority of our residents have been active in their churches before coming to Holly Hall. However, the good feeling of being welcomed into CLE as a caring fellowship may be strongest in the lives of those who have not been active in church for some years before making the move to Holly Hall. New residents who have been active in their own churches tend, at first, to shy away from what they interpret as a duplication of "church" at Holly Hall. They do not think of themselves as being ready for church "at home" and still think in terms of "going to church." It is obvious, of course, that as men and women pass out of that sphere of worship Paul Hoon has described as "relevant" (that which affirms the worldly meaning of existence), they become more capable (although it does not happen automatically) of experiencing "worship as irrelevance that crucifies the world and summons [us] to count all things as loss that [we] may gain Christ." [5] This is part of the need we have for a gradual simplification of life which, in turn, provides an opportunity for growth in the faith of the resurrection that is gloriously irrelevant when compared to how some senior citizens' groups become dry appendages to full congregational life. It helps to define the New Testament hope described by Dietrich Bonhoeffer as "the beyond in the midst of life." The joy inspired by this concept may indeed sum up the intentionality of God's creation. However, I must add that participation in Christian Life Emphasis at Holly Hall puts residents in touch with each other in such meaningful ways that it often enables those who have undergone pronounced disengagement losses to experience once again "worship as relevance." When that takes place, I find singing the Doxology to be the most fitting response.

We look forward to the possibility that our experiences of prayer and praise may, in time, help many of God's people to discover the freedom of old age. How successfully this is achieved depends, to some extent, on whether the community understands these experiences as an expression of liberation. It is my contention that the elderly, like the poor, may be regarded as those who, as marginalized people, must act out "a new way of living and thinking the faith, a new way of being summoned and summoning into *ecclesia*." [6]

Chapter 9

Weakness as an Acceptable Sacrifice

My grace is sufficient for you, for my power is made perfect in weakness.
— 2 Corinthians 12:9a

Lent

In order for people of advanced years and declining vitality to know that we really do care for them as individuals, we must be sufficiently humble in the sight of God to be able truthfully to minister in love and kindness to their needs. It is unfortunate that some of the things we must do in order to ensure that each resident is receiving the care that he or she really needs, are perceived as arbitrary and abusive of authority. Because the proper utilization of rooms within the retirement complex demands that levels of care be established, we cannot escape that charge. If we want to obtain the best possible response to our decision-making, it is important that we routinely be viewed as those who put a high priority upon patience and long suffering in our relationships with those who are, in varying degrees, our responsibility. I do not suppose that I will ever get used to having to move someone who has passed the point of being able to understand why the move has to be made.

The fact that I am an ordained minister is an advantage most of the time in being able to maintain a high level of trust with the residents. However, it becomes the main point of attack when anyone feels as if I have treated them unfairly. In being viewed as the cause of their frustration and, in a sense, humiliation, I nonetheless seek to identify with them in the struggle they are waging against being thrust even further away from the mainstream of life. I search for some glimmer of hope for those who are forced to take up residence at the far end of the housing continuum. In the process of my search, I find that those who are not overcome with disappointment are given, through Christ, a power that is made perfect in weakness. It is made known in a ministry of grace that bids the strong to become weak for the sake of the Gospel.

When we assume the emptiness of worldly power, we open ourselves to the possibility of being granted spiritual power. However, it is important to realize that we obtain spiritual power only as a gift of God. It is not an automatic consequence of weakness, just as it is not an automatic reward for good work. Then we are able to keep it only as we give it away, unselfconsciously, to bless the lives of others. We lose it the moment that it becomes a source of pride or a lever to gain special favors. I have witnessed tactics of intimidation whereby those who are weak in body seek to keep or to gain control over the lives of certain family members. This can be a source of great pain for those who really care about the older person but who, nonetheless, grow weary of always being at their beck and call.

I have chosen to write, in some detail, about my experience of learning what it is like to be disabled in the manner of those who occupy rooms in the Health Center. I do so in the belief that we should gain as much knowledge as possible about what life offers each day and night to those for whom we have a service responsibility. It has become clear to me that being with them, in their midst, and being instructed by them, enables our liturgy to be a work of the people. The meaning of this for the faith we profess was captured in the words of Stanley Hauerwas when he described the Church as "God's gesture through which we may have a foretaste of the Kingdom...to hear and retell the story is to bend the body." [7] It is amazing what flows from my experience of ministry that this expression so aptly defines.

Good Friday

Good Friday was a day of chaos and confusion at Holly Hall. First, a foundation repair company got an early morning start on drilling large holes along the office corridor inside the building. The sound was deafening. The building shook. Telephone conversation was impossible. Then, in the early afternoon, death came to one of our residents on the D-Wing of the Health Center. I visited with the brother of the deceased, who came quickly after he was called. We planned a Memorial Service in the Chapel for the following Tuesday morning. All at once, without a chance to catch my breath, it was time for our 2:45 p.m. Good Friday service. The residents, inconvenienced once again, had to be directed single file down half of the corridor while, on the other half, large wheelbarrows burdened with concrete were rolling along.

That particular Good Friday was to be significant for me in another way. I was preparing myself for the experience of being a resident in our full nursing care area known, at that time, as the Infirmary. It had taken me quite awhile to make up my mind to go through with the plan. The idea for it came about as a mild challenge from Dr. David Oliver who, at the time, was my faculty consultant on D.Min. studies at St. Paul School of Theology. I went through all kinds of excuses not to do it. I really did not want, as the Administrator of Holly Hall, to be exposed to such indignity. Finally, my excuses became the best reasons for accepting the challenge. It also occurred to me that to enter into such confinement—to "go down"—on Good Friday would give a powerful faith meaning to the twenty-four hour experience.

Once I had made the decision to go through with it, I immediately began to feel the hurt of what was coming. I thought of the scriptural accounts of the events leading up to the trial and crucifixion of Jesus. I thought of the steadfastness with which he set his face to go to Jerusalem. The deprivation that I was about to feel was not really all that important. But by identifying with these special people, at the place where they spend all of their hours, I hoped to find meaning in the weakness and vulnerability of their condition.

Following a brief explanation to the residents of what I was about to do, I pronounced the benediction and walked back to a wheelchair, removed my robe and tie, and was pushed to the Infirmary by Elaine Geist, the Assistant Administrator, where I was admitted as a resident into Room B-10.

I had set it up so that I could not support my weight on my legs. I had to be lifted in and out of the wheelchair. Two of the residents who visited regularly in the nursing care section came to see me. One of them recited a poem and the other one offered a prayer. I was touched by the spiritually uplifting character of their caring ministry. Later in the evening, I heard a man playing dominoes with his mother. It was impossible not to follow the one-sided conversation:

"Mother, it's your move."
"Mother, we've got a spinner."
"You're ten points behind, Mother."
"I domino, Mother."
"You beat me by five, Mother."
"You're a good scout, Mother."
Finally, beautifully, "I love you, Mother."

Then I heard the medication cart as it came slowly up the corridor. I heard my own mind asking, "Why?" I thought about Jesus' words in John's Gospel, "No one takes my life from me. I lay it down of my own accord." I thought to myself, "No one is making me do this."

The two Nurses' Aides who assisted me to bed on Friday evening were real pros. They took care of everything quickly and efficiently. My sleep that night, however, was not good. I kept hearing noises in the hallway. Then I was awakened by the L.V.N. checking the room. Not long after that an Aide came in, turned on the light, and took my vital signs. I used the urinal bottle that was hooked to the bed rail. Early Saturday morning, I heard a resident from C-Wing cry out. It was a stroke victim who had enjoyed painting when she first came into Holly Hall several years before. A little later I heard a man call, "Bring me something to eat." He had been a baseball pitcher in the early years of his life. Sounds of the morning activity could be heard all around. The two young Nurses' Aides who had to lift me out of bed had a hard time with their feelings. One of them could not keep from giggling. Getting me on and off the commode following breakfast was particularly tedious and embarrassing. They almost dropped me as they were trying to get me back into the wheelchair.

The morning moved along rather quickly. I made notes and turned in every direction for variety. I read the Gospel of John and listened to two of Bach's greatest pieces of music (the only two items I allowed myself for diversion and inspiration). The food was good and I was pleased with the service that was performed by the Holly Hall employees. I am grateful that the majority of those who cannot claim executive privilege feel the same way.

Some thoughts concerning my experience that I feel are worth sharing include the following:

1) *It is so easy to hang the head.* I see it so much that I found myself copying the look. However, I must say that it is tiring to

hold the upper body erect for very long. And, with the interruptions of sleep at night, chair dozing throughout the day occurs easily and frequently. But the slumping posture also denotes a certain amount of shame in not being able to stand tall. Those who are in wheelchairs have a hard time maintaining their self-esteem. This becomes an even greater challenge when visitors persistently talk down to them from a standing position.

2) *I became aware of every aspect of my immediate surroundings.* I did absolutely nothing for long periods of time, trying to determine what meaning, if any, I could derive from just *being*. At first, I became aware of every spot on the wall where fresh paint was needed. I saw every bit of dust that had been left in a corner. I noted a blind that needed minor repairs. I felt anger, disgust, sadness and depression. Only as I, with my mind, was able to move outside of the room, or when others were in the room, did those feelings subside. I realized the value of being able to move about, of seeing different people and of engaging them in conversation. I realized how important possessions are to those whose possessions have been reduced to a very few items. I remembered how frequently I had spoken to others about the importance of simplifying life by getting rid of the "things" they no longer need.

3) *I determined that being confined to a wheelchair forces an acute awareness of bodily functions.* I understood, at last, why residents in wheelchairs so often want to be put to bed ahead of

schedule. They get tired and the body stiffens in its sitting position to the extent that the bed provides welcome relief. It allows stretching out in every direction. Also, we come to terms with the body very quickly when its functions become sluggish or uncomfortable. Those of us who do not regularly live with incontinence or even the more common problems of deafness or failing vision, cannot really appreciate what accommodations have to be made in order to get through each day. We are challenged as Christians to value the body within the unity of personhood whereby we sense the image of God. If the limiting aspects of the aging body are allowed to shape what others think about the aging process and what the frail elderly think about themselves, we will be in danger of perpetuating the dualism (made popular in Greek philosophy) which depicts the body as valueless.

Notes from Saturday Evening

Away from the Infirmary, reflecting upon my experience, I felt both joy and sadness, along with some guilt. There was joy over having accomplished what I did. There was sadness because of the loneliness and confusion that exists in such a setting. There was a slight feeling of guilt for having feigned weakness. I felt compassion for those who had waited on me as if I really had been incapacitated. The memory of the Nurses' Aide kneeling on the floor to put on my socks and shoes would not be easily forgotten.

Easter

Our celebration of the resurrection that year was like no other that I had ever experienced. I had been, at that time, in the pulpit of the Holly Hall Chapel every Easter Sunday morning for sixteen years. Never before had I been as personally affected. I felt released into the world. I had been raised from a state of dependence and weakness. Having gone through the lowering sense of being subject, briefly, to the powers of death, I could discern the eternal weight of glory wherein light eclipses darkness and the full harmony of joy replaces the discordant notes of decline and despair. My spirit was overflowing with Good News and the congregation was with me all the way. In praying for the members of our community who could not walk away from where they were, I asked that Christ's victory over death might give them hope in their waiting and that they might know that God waits, anticipating for them the *parousia*...that journey's end uniting that will gather all that they have been into all that they will be.

Eastertide Reflections

I am amazed at the power that a sense of personhood can continue to convey to the oldest of the old. The capacity to recall where one has been and what one has done stays with the majority long after physical strength is gone. The memory of particular life events is important for self-affirmation. So many of these people are telling us, "I will tell you my story if you will only pause long enough to hear it." They have been conditioned to believe that they are not important enough to elicit a boldness in anyone to approach their memory and desire with any degree of seriousness. The price to be paid in accepting the challenge is in the minutes that we say we do not have in sufficient number.

Weakness as an acceptable sacrifice is a weakness that, at its heart, is strong enough to delay death without that being the deliberate intention. On the other hand, I have known a few—very few—who, in their weakness, seemed to will death and, in the strength of that desire, helped to make it come true. As God claims the sacrifice of that which most closely approximates our state of being, we find ourselves impulsing the scriptural holiness described by Charles Wesley in the words of one of his many hymns:

In want my plentiful supply,
In weakness my almighty power,
In bonds my perfect liberty,
My light in Satan's darkest hour,
In grief my joy unspeakable
My life in death, my heaven in hell.

The final chapter of our aging, as Christians conditioned through life by the "hidden source of calm repose," can be a monument to "pure, unbounded love." Trembling on the brink of eternity, like deeply ripened fruit ready to drop from the tree, we are known and loved as individuals by the God whose hands have shaped us and whose will is finally to make us perfect. Again, we are instructed by Charles Wesley:

Finish, then, thy new creation;
Pure and spotless let us be.
Let us see thy great salvation
Perfectly restored in thee:
Changed from glory into glory,
Till in heaven we take our place,
Till we cast our crowns before thee,
Lost in wonder, love, and praise.

Chapter 10

Preparing to Go Home

Lord, make me to know mine end,
and the measure of my days, what it is;
that I may know how frail I am.
—Psalm 39:4, KJV

Life's a voyage that's homeward bound.
—Herman Melville

The word "home" is symbolic of a multitude of feelings and emotions concerning love, protection, warmth and well-being. Nursing Home residents who are tired of their narrow routine of existence cry out for "home." Many times in our Holly Hall Infirmary I have heard the plaintive entreaty, "I want to go home." The concept of home also is associated with thoughts and visions of a heavenly home where all is peace and joy and where pain and sorrow will be no more. Within this eternal dwelling place, in the general Christian perspective, there is God, known by many as the Heavenly Father, who waits to bestow a special blessing upon those who have waited, sometimes for many years, for the call to "come home."

It is the idea of someone special who waits that makes the idea of home so meaningful. Who among us is there who, after returning home after an absence of any duration, does not rejoice in the welcome received from family members? As I return from the assortment of things that I have had to do during the day, I never fail to appreciate the greeting I receive from family members who are already there. Although not all home-comings are happy, the thought of "going home" is, most often, a pleasant prospect.

In the Scriptures there are homecomings of special significance. None of them more closely approximates the concept of ultimate welcome than that of the story of the prodigal son in Luke's Gospel. What a beautiful picture of unconditional love! A son who has foolishly squandered his inheritance and who has exhibited such impetuous and immature behavior is being welcomed in such a royal manner. This is the receptivity of the parent who is like God, who offers forgiveness to the wanderer and who restores him to a place of honor in the household. "See what love the Father has given us, that we should be called the children of God" (1 John 3:1). This is part of the meaning of that eternal beckoning that penetrates the gloom and sadness of life's final farewells. It is the ultimate gift of faith as it blesses the lives of those who are called "home" to where God, the divine Parent, waits in anticipation of each child's return.

I have been privileged, during my ministry, to walk with a number of courageous people right up to that valley of the shadow through which they were called to pass before experiencing the joy reserved for God's faithful servants. It is a humbling responsibility. Since being at Holly Hall, this particular aspect of pastoral concern has focused on the elderly person who slowly or with occasional and surprising swiftness moves past the boundaries of this life.

When accompanying an older person up to the "valley of the shadow of death," holding the hand is a very important gesture of comfort and indication of a caring presence. I have been amazed at the strength of one who has been bed-ridden for months as they grasp the hand of one whom they recognize as a special friend. I have been surprised by the verbal responses from those who have been at death's door. This was true when I went to see one of our residents who had been hospitalized with a stroke. She had not spoken to anyone for several days. The nursing attendant who had been with her on the same shift for most of the time was amazed to hear her trying to speak after I reached her bed and told her my name. When, upon preparing to leave, I said, "God bless you," and received a clear reply, "God bless you," the attendant, undoubtedly a person of strong religious persuasion, cried out, "Praise the Lord!"

There is not an unusual preoccupation with death at Holly Hall. Most of the residents are conscious of it hovering near but are not excessively alarmed by it—not nearly so much as the fear of having to linger here in some semi-conscious state without the power to reason or to enjoy life in any way. Many express a desire to be able to quietly fall asleep. They realize, however, that they cannot determine when or how death will come. It is true that we cannot understand why God waits to release certain people from an existence of suffering and despair. Perhaps, in the same way, Christians have sought to understand the bitter agony of Christ upon the cross. The assurance rests on the promise that, beyond all of the grief of lingering in the body after meaningful life has passed, God waits, with a divine sorrow, and that it is God who will, at last, set all things straight.

In the daily responsibility of serving the needs of the Holly Hall residents, there are particular chores and instructive conversations that deal with the preparation for and the facing of death. A good number of the residents recognize that it will be helpful if they make plans for their funeral. Sometimes, family members will not allow them to talk about such preparations. Some of the residents, on their own, secure pre-paid burial plans in order to save on the already high cost of dying. Some of them circumvent such high costs by donating their bodies for medical research. Occasionally some will come up with a change in plans. Sadly, there are instances when they find themselves mourning the death of adult children. These losses often are hard to overcome. Every now and then a minister whom they had hoped would be able to conduct their funeral service no longer is available because of death or retirement. In other instances, they may not have seen a minister from their church in years. This is how it happens that I am called upon to officiate at many of the services for members of our Holly Hall family.

I have had funeral and memorial services for residents of Holly Hall in a variety of situations, from the worship settings of large churches to the rather impersonal funeral home chapels, from being the only minister in rural churches and cemeteries to services with one or more other ministers in chapel or sanctuary. Sometimes there are graveside services only. The residents appreciate the memorial services that are held in the Holly Hall Chapel, since it permits so many more of them to attend.

On a cold winter day, I had a service for the ship captain's widow. Her name was Shirley Waters. Only the Funeral Director was there with me. Her ashes were scattered over Galveston Bay. Then, on a warm summer day, my wife and I drove to the East Texas town of Athens for a graveside service for Mrs. Alice Thomas. She had shown me pictures of the cemetery site. It was sheltered by two large magnolia trees that she and her sister had planted following the death of her husband many years before. Although the temperature was in the high 80s, we felt an amazing coolness the moment we entered the shade of those magnificent trees. I compared that sensation, as I spoke to the people, to passage from the feverish heat of this world to the coolness and balm of God's eternal dwelling place.

I take with complete seriousness each opportunity I have to affirm the life of one who has lived at Holly Hall. In the spirit of the "Gospel's joyful sound," I borrow thoughts from the relationship that the staff and residents have had with the deceased in order to bring to mind her or his special contribution to our life together. These insights may not be as available to a pastor who has not known the resident as long or as well. However, I must make it clear that I appreciate the long-standing tie some residents maintain with the church of their membership that enables them to be supported, through death, by the caring ministry of the congregation.

I seek to provide a reasonable response to the problem described by some residents as a feeling of uselessness. I try to convey a spirit of hope in reply to each question that is asked with a sigh of resignation or despair. Sometimes the residents provide the best answers to their own questions. They say, "God must have some reason for keeping me here." I add an encouraging word when such statements are made, trying to lift them a little higher and to help them to see how they may engage those who live around them in some form of spiritually meaningful communication. It happens, of course, that no matter how strong the desire and the effort, the day will come when the senses will grow dim and the limbs will grow weak. Then we may call it a blessing of God when they are summoned home.

I have seen several instances of heroic existence at Holly Hall prior to death. One situation in which I was particularly involved because there were no family members to assist was that of a man far past 90 years of age and his wife who was just a few years younger. The man had an artificial leg and was deaf. His wife was able to communicate with him as no one else could. They shared the sorrow of having lost their only child, a son, just after his graduation from college. It was said by some who knew them that the father became bitter and reclusive after his son's death. Sometimes the wife would push the husband in a wheelchair and sometimes (always to and from the dining room) he would push her. With stoic fortitude she would tend to all of the little personal chores necessary for their simple existence in the area where minimal nursing assistance is provided. He did not like it when she was away from him for very long. It was a hot, early summer day when I took this faithful wife to Methodist Hospital. I had the nurse put a few of her things in a suitcase. She made it clear to her husband where she was going, having put it off for as long as she could. The pain had, at last, become too great for her to bear.

I visited this dear lady in the hospital. She would inquire about her husband and ask me to send him her love. I printed messages for him to read. He accepted my visits, and the concern I had for both of them, with genuine appreciation. His wife rallied briefly and then, as often seems the case, lost the battle. I'm sure that her days were extended by virtue of her strong desire not to have to leave her husband alone. I knew that it would be difficult having to break the news to the one whose life she had shared for so many years. I was prepared to sit with him longer than usual. I printed a note, as was my custom. This time there was one word that told it all. He accepted the news with a determined effort not to cry. He seemed to have a need to remain reserved and unemotional. Yet, as I shook his hand and heard his "thank you" in a accent revealing his earliest days as a native of Great Britain, I saw the tears in his eyes. This would be a ritual of parting that we would repeat each time I left his room thereafter for as long as he was aware of my presence.

I arranged for his wife's funeral through the Episcopal Church of which they were members and the Funeral Home that they had chosen long before. Upon returning to the hospital to pick up the suitcase that belonged to them, I noticed a tag attached to the handle with the words printed on it, "Wesley Stevens—Friend—Holly Hall." After such a long life these words spoke of the reduction, at the end, to a few simple reminders of this earthly journey and a friend who would carry her suitcase back to Holly Hall. In October of that same year, her husband, a man of few words but very deep thoughts, quietly slipped away. I can still see his moist eyes and hear his crisp British "thank you."

The following stories, describing the last days of three ladies I have known, are told as examples of how time has changed the way many people have to die.

Story #1

I think, first of all, of my grandmother who, during her last days, engaged in a ritual of constantly turning small objects in her aproned lap. This activity of her fingers served as a tactile reminder of her seasons of labor in a world far removed from the high cost of preserving life. As she revisioned the past, in the warm afternoons of her last summer, she also previsioned the future, softly humming:

There's a land that is fairer than day
And by faith we can see it afar.

She and my grandfather kept visiting preachers in their home, discussing the price of oats and the prospects of rain with greater urgency than the prophecies of Jeremiah or the parables of Jesus. At their times of worship, in the church across the river, the preacher sometimes would ask, "Sister Shuptrine, will you lead us in prayer?" before expounding from the pulpit on the gift of salvation.

Then, one morning at the breakfast table, Grandmother Shuptrine bowed her head and, in the company of family, quietly "fell asleep," inheriting the promise after "having greeted it from afar."

Story #2

In the early seventies, at Holly Hall, a resident went into a coma following a stroke. She remained in a mostly unconscious state for almost two years. During that time she was tube fed and given close and attentive care by the nursing department. Her daughter, unable to handle her mother's condition, moved out of the state in order not to feel an obligation to visit with any frequency. She would telephone us from time to time in order to receive the news that there was no change.

The cost of this lady's care, with the exception of a small old-age pension, was subsidized by Holly Hall. Holly Hall, with caring hands, reached out daily to this person, a child of God, invoking God's watchful care upon one who could offer us nothing in return except a personal presence reminding us of both the fragile and the enduring aspects of life.

A respiratory complication gave the attending physician reason to discuss with me the desirability of a treatment beyond what had been routinely administered. I knew him to be one in whom the Spirit of God had made particular inroads. In prayerful respect for the thin thread that had kept Mrs. H. in a state of survival for so long, we nonetheless concluded, under the circumstances, that her movement into the fulness of God's presence should not be delayed by heroic medical effort.

Story #3

In the antiseptic hospital room designated as ICU, where a variety of codes offer their respective calls to appropriate activity on behalf of those who are kept alive by lengths of tubes connecting them to monitors of sophisticated design, a Holly Hall resident was separated, except for brief visitation intervals, from those who loved her. In anguish over her condition, and the ethical dilemma surrounding it, the family proceeded to talk with anyone who might be able to suggest what course of action should be followed. While they were not people who expressed great concern over the expense that was involved in prolonging their loved one's life, they certainly were aware of the charges that were accumulating with each passing day. It was difficult, in my thinking, to relate prayer to the procedures by which everyone involved was, in a sense, victimized. The story of the patient's life, as a source of prayerful reflection, was hard to focus upon because of the seemingly inevitable course of medical intervention that was keeping her alive. Even the room of the Holly Hall Infirmary, where the previously described drama of lingering life was played out, seemed much less impersonal. I realize, of course, that the conditions were not alike. In the case where the resident was able to remain at Holly Hall, the cost of care was not a concern and the moral issue was not as complicated.

After several emotionally draining weeks for the family of the hospitalized resident, there was recovery sufficient to transfer her to a medically acceptable nursing care center where the proper equipment was available to sustain her life. Even then, there was very little hope. Tears of thanksgiving came when, after only a few days, our Holly Hall friend was released from her tenuous hold upon life.

God's goodness and mercy surely was with each one of these ladies as they approached the end of their days upon the earth. But, if a choice were possible, who among us would not choose the way my grandmother was allowed, in quiet dignity, to leave this world?

We spend our time with those whose days have narrowed down to a few in number, trusting that our labor is not in vain, trusting that we are contributing to the building up of the Body of Christ. All the while, we rejoice in the assurance of God's Word, "Inasmuch as ye have done it unto one of the least of these my brethren, ye have done it unto me" (Matt. 25:40, KJV).

At Last, For Me

If I must face a period of time in which I will not be able to attend worship because of the infirmities of old age, I pray that I will be surrounded by faithful witnesses to the God of Israel and Jesus. I want to be reminded of my baptism and I want to celebrate, with others as much as possible, Holy Communion. I want to listen to great music (majestic hymns of faith) as a doxological component of worshiping with the saints "in spirit and in truth." I pray for safe lodging and peace at the end with someone left who will be able, and truthfully willing, to affirm my life in such a way that God's Name will be praised.

Chapter 11

Last Laughter

He laughs best who laughs last.
—Sir John Vanbrugh

I feel reasonably sure that when Sir John Vanbrugh wrote the words quoted above, he was not thinking about the laughter that comes during the last days of life. However, that quotation, even if it is lifted out of its original meaning, has much to commend its attachment to the laughter of those who face imminent departure from this earth. The older person who is able to laugh is likely to be one whose company people of all ages enjoy.

Laughter, as it comes to those with whom we work day by day, often emerges out of the various incidents of life that are perceived as humorous by the residents themselves. We are permitted, at times, to laugh with them, but some of the things they find very funny are things that either may not strike a younger person as being all that laugh-provoking, or may be something at which we dare not laugh, not yet belonging to the circle of those who are entitled to laugh at each other's stories concerning the annoyances and confusion of growing old. This laughter centers around losses. It is brave laughter, since it defies the trials of life by making light of them. Laughing in the face of death reduces the dread of its sting and, what is more, it helps to provide strength to endure the slights and injustices that accompany senescence. Also, it is a far better alternative than pretending, in morose silence, that "these things" are not real or than in crying out in abject despair over what being alive so long causes.

The laughter we witness possesses a sense of carefree abandonment not unlike that which is associated with losing control. However, it does not arise out of an "eat, drink and be merry for tomorrow we may die" kind of existence. It is a course of Christian living charted by a dead reckoning of divine origin through which victory is obtained over the powers that deprive life of deeply human responses—including laughter. Those who are able to lose themselves in soul-refreshing laughter are experiencing a fruit of the Spirit. It allows each one of us to be closer to God and to each other by drawing out the child that lives inside us. It has been described by one from whom I have gained much spiritual insight as being "wrapped in the Good News so kindly that the Mickey Mouse in your soul will never die."

Note: Laughter in any age is good medicine and, therefore, what I am saying should not be judged as categorically exclusive of the simple pleasures anyone gains from experiencing something that brings on laughter—happy, uproarious or inward laughter.

A lady called to talk with me about coming to Holly Hall. She was in a pleasant frame of mind. I knew her to be a Christian. She began by telling me that her house had sold and that she now was facing the task of getting rid of "thousands of things" in anticipation of moving into smaller quarters at Holly Hall. She said, "My friends keep asking me how I can, all at once, get rid of the things I have accumulated over 54 years." I said to her, "You should tell them, 'How can I not get rid of them?'" The sound of her laughter over the telephone told me that she knew exactly what I meant. It was laughing in the face of a change happily anticipated as the logical "next step" in a life that had followed a positive track all of her days.

I do regret that I have not been able, in this narrative, to do justice to the humorous aspect of life at Holly Hall that is such a vital part of the lives of the residents. However, it is difficult to convey in writing. Also, it might be misunderstood. I would not want anyone to think that I was making fun of the residents or the problems of growing old.

So we laugh along with the residents. We laugh at certain jokes and statements that we know are intended to make us laugh. Sometimes we may laugh later when we think back upon an incident that turned out to be funny even though that was not the intention at the time it happened. We laughed when a gentleman who was almost blind was asked by a lady in the hallway, "Are you looking for me?" and he replied, "I don't know, what do you look like?" I remember when I had to glue Joseph's head back on. (A resident brought the ceramic figures of Mary and Joseph to my office. Joseph had met with an accident.) We laughed over whether she should keep Mary or whether Mary would stay with Joseph during his convalescence. Then, when I returned Joseph to her, we had to look for the baby

Jesus, who had gotten lost, before the Holy Family was at last reunited.

It's just that I did not want to write the last word without emphasizing the significance of last laughter and giving it credit, even though it cannot be documented adequately, for helping all of us. Again, it is the ingredient that can make advanced age less burdensome and those who fit that category more enjoyable to be around. It illustrates, in moments of unselfconscious pleasure, the grace that can accompany "letting go." If you should decide to grow old along with me at Holly Hall, be sure to bring along some laughter or, at least, a smile. You just might not be admitted without it.

Grow old along with me!
The best is yet to be,
The last of life,
for which the first was made.
Our times are in his hand
Who saith, "A while I planned;
Youth shows but half. Trust God;
see all; nor be afraid!"[8]
— Robert Browning

Postscript

Retirement living, in settings designed for those who have determined that it is best for them to live around and with those of their own age and interest, is in a state of remarkable growth. During the years following the time when the earlier chapters of this book were written, there have been many new and attractive places built to house the nation's older population. Most of them have incorporated various amenities in order to attract those who are able to pay higher fees. The competition in the retirement housing market has become fairly intense.

In former days, Holly Hall's attraction was such that a waiting period of up to three years was faced by those seeking admission. That began to change in the early 80s. A gradual decline in interest by the people traditionally served by Holly Hall resulted primarily from outdated physical facilities. Residents had to go down the hall to take baths. Foundation shifting caused cracking walls. The hallway lighting was poor and a variety of heating and cooling systems, including window units, were in constant need of repair. Those who came with the idea of applying for admission often were disappointed at what they saw. However, those who completed the application and were accepted for admission realized, soon after moving in, that they had made the right choice. They appreciated the concern that was shown for the needs of each resident. They enjoyed the good food and they readily identified with the community spirit. They boasted that they had the best place in town to live.

In any event, the Board of Directors of Holly Hall made the decision to have a master plan of renovation drawn up by an architectural firm. This resulted, subsequently, in a contract being awarded. The projected expense for everything that would be done was close to six million dollars.

Renovation featured an attractive new roof line over the independent living corridors. It included a new system of air-conditioning with individual controls in each resident's room. A complete bath was added to each room. Carpet was installed over almost all of the old floor space. New and renewed dining rooms were occupied by the residents with exclamations of awe and wonder. Freshly furnished living areas popped up all over the building. The "city within a city" concept, developed by the architects, turned a section of former resident rooms into space for a new beauty shop, library, post office and a room for private parties or small group meetings.

New construction created additional independent living with two atrium clusters consisting of twenty-five efficiency apartments. A link was built connecting these units to the Activities Building and to the renovated corridors. A new Service building, facilities for housekeeping, laundry and maintenance, and a new administrative office configuration were added.

A special donation allowed for renovation of the existing Activities Building. The new functional design divided the building into two sections, one for crafts and one for large group meetings and a variety of programs and entertainment. Other features of the project included a prominently located greenhouse, a wood working shop, a large section of loop road within the newly landscaped grounds and a walking path with exercise stations. Increased safety features and new security gates were a part of the general plan of improvements. The expectations centered around being able to attract the active retired person to Holly Hall.

A Capital Campaign to raise funds for such an extensive project was quite successful. People in Houston who, through the years, had known about and supported Holly Hall were quite generous. The Board of Directors, as expected, provided the impetus and the working leadership for the Campaign.

It is evident, at this point, that Holly Hall is poised on the brink of a new era. The news has gone out to the churches that something important for their members to consider is taking place on the twenty acres across from the Astrodome.

All of this is to emphasize, in a broader context, that continuing care retirement communities which were built over twenty-five years ago must face the necessity of change in order for them to continue to exist. Non-profit organizations, such as Holly Hall, must find that middle ground of caring services and facility improvement balanced against the careful use of operating revenue. This is important, on the one hand, in order to attract a sufficient number of full paying residents and, on the other hand, to be able to accept qualified residents who cannot afford to pay the full cost of care. It is sad to think that housing for the modest income elderly may be the hardest to sustain. The funding requirements of such housing may, in the future, severely limit the amount of subsidized care that we are able to offer. But, whatever the future holds, Holly Hall is committed, in the spirit of Christian love, to the fulfillment of the often used motto, "to add years to life and life to years" for an interesting variety of people who choose and are chosen for residency.

Appendix A
Rituals of Belonging

A Commitment to Christian Life Emphasis (CLE) as a Resident of Holly Hall

1. To commit myself to the study of Scripture each day in accordance with a specific lectionary

2. To commit myself to prayer and meditation on the Christian life each day

3. To maintain loyalty to the church of my baptism/membership

4. To assist in Christian worship and service at Holly Hall by:

    a. Attendance upon services of worship

    b. Assistance, as I am able, in preparing and conducting worship services

c. Evidence of Christian concern for all of God's people who live and work at Holly Hall

d. Assistance in the process of bringing others into the caring, serving community of faith at Holly Hall

5. To resist idleness and boredom through both structured and unstructured activities, including study and visitation. Also, to find ways to order my life so that, spiritually, I may be in tune with God's ultimate purpose for me.

____

Signature

The Blessing of a Room
For Occupancy by a New Resident of Holly Hall

Resident/Leader: We gather here to welcome a new friend, ________________, into Holly Hall and to ask God's blessing upon this room prepared for her use. We are thankful for the freedom we have as individuals and yet we celebrate the faith and love that binds us together as a family of God in this place.

Resident/Participant: In the Book of Proverbs we read: "By wisdom a house is built, and by understanding it is established. By knowledge the rooms are filled with all precious and pleasant riches."

Unison Response: GLORY BE TO GOD!

Administrator/Minister: As in baptism we entered the care and keeping of God through the Church, so, by this ceremony, do we acknowledge your entry into the special, caring ministry of Holly Hall.

Let us pray. Almighty God, whose Son Jesus did, by his presence, bless the house in Bethany of Mary and Martha and their brother Lazarus; bless, we pray, this house of many rooms, that it might be a haven of blessing and a place of peace. As Room ______ has sheltered others, now let it be dedicated anew for the use of ____________________, through Jesus Christ our Lord. Amen.

A SERVICE OF ACCEPTANCE FOR A NEW RESIDENT OF HOLLY HALL (FOLLOWING PROBATION)

Resident/Leader:	Inasmuch as our friend, _________ , has been a resident of Holly Hall for three months, we come today to acknowledge the end of her probation and to give her thanks for God's watchful care over her.
Resident/Participant:	As God established a covenant with Israel and said to David, "I will appoint a place for my people Israel, and will plant them, that they may dwell in their own place and be disturbed no more," we rejoice that __________ may now dwell at Holly Hall in peace.
Unison Response:	YOU ARE ACCEPTED! THANKS BE TO GOD!
Administrator/Minister:	As in confirmation you accepted the place established for you among the people of God, so by this ceremony

do we acknowledge the commencement of your days as a fully accepted member of the Holly Hall family of residents.

Let us pray.

Almighty God, whose providential care has brought ________ to Holly Hall, we are thankful for her acceptance into this caring fellowship. Bless her life at Holly Hall. Grant her, we pray, pleasant days, the companionship of good friends and, always, the presence of your Spirit, through Jesus Christ our Lord. Amen.

Appendix B
Notes on Nursing Care Communion

Kingdomtide

This morning we started using the intinction method to serve communion to our frail elderly residents. It is far more practical that the little cups and it possesses such powerful symbolism of the grace of God. The movement of the service succeeds in encompassing the full range of eucharistic worship and, along with a spiritual awareness of God's presence, achieves a degree of acceptance that is inspiring to behold. It reveals a community of faith.

The necessity of staff and others to occasionally "pass through" the service in progress adds to the element of the sacramental set down in the midst of other essential activities. It reminds me of the theme of James White's book, *The Worldliness of Worship*. As my consultant in the area of Christian worship, Larry Wagley, wrote to me concerning the setting of this service across from the kitchen and close to resident rooms, "That literally moves the meal closer to the people and gives the service an integrity sometimes lacking in church."

During the service today, a Lab Technician came to take blood from one of the residents. What an amazing coincidence! While the blood of physical life was being taken, the blood that identifies us with life in Christ was being given.

We are presented with various illustrations of how the Spirit of God moves into the horizontal dimension of routine care that is symbolic of the unity of body and soul. One aspect of care is not elevated in such a way that makes other aspects of care seem secondary in importance. This speaks of the truth of the faith embodied in the assertion from John's Gospel, "The Word became flesh and dwelt among us."

Epiphany

The Nursing Care Communion at Holly Hall continues to be a special time of reaching out in Christian love to those who are "down." A powerful symbolism of grace is manifested in the passing of the peace and in having the bread and wine, by intinction, placed into the mouth of each communicant. Through the repetition of this simple design for Christian eucharistic worship, the frail elderly acknowledge their acceptance by the manner in which they receive the blessing of Christ's presence.

As we made our way down the line today, one of the residents, who is undergoing the additional anxiety of treatment for cancer, exhibited misgivings over receiving the sacrament as we approached her. She shook her head from side to side as if she did not wish to partake. Moving on, we went into the D-Wing where we delivered the bread and wine to two residents, one of whom was bed-ridden. As we turned to go back from where we had come, we saw the resident we had so recently by-passed coming toward us in her wheelchair. She had her mouth open! Somehow, she realized what she had missed and was coming after it! No words were spoken. We paused . the bread was placed in her mouth . she appeared to be at peace.

Advent

The Nursing Care Communion establishes a tone of deep spirituality. Even in its simplicity it reenacts the historical purposes of the Sacrament. Participants, including an occasional visiting family member, often are moved to tears during the "passing of the peace." The greetings we receive from the residents are indicative, not just of their recognition of us, but of what, or who, it is we represent. We carry a message to them from beyond us, but it is embodied in the person of each one of us who have been given the burden and the glory of such exalted self-emptying. Dwelling along the margin of the river of life we receive the Body of the Lord Jesus Christ broken for us and thereby receive Christ's identification with our brokenness.

A gentleman was with us in the nursing care communion for the first time. He had sustained injuries from a fall in the cottage where he lived with his wife. He had been a member of his church choir for many years. He contributed to the singing and following the benediction he smiled and said, "That was a good service." Not many days later, he died quietly in his room after enjoying a pleasant visit with some special friends. I thought of the Eucharist as it is celebrated in anticipation of the completion of all things in Jesus Christ.

Appendix C
Incidents Generated by the CLE Influence

1. A resident returned from the hospital very happy that her problem was not nearly as serious as was initially feared. She wanted to share her feeling of thanksgiving with friends at Holly Hall. She called the Chairperson of the CLE Council and asked if she would invite a few people to her room and provide the leadership for a time of prayerful thanksgiving. I was asked to attend. Three of us met in the resident's room. Each one made a contribution. The comments and prayers spoke in a meaningful way to the need of this person. She was very happy as a result of the initiative she took to bring others into her room to share her joy.

2. Following the Nursing Care Communion, the two residents from Independent Living who had been appointed to assist in that service were walking back down the corridor to their rooms. Miss Frances Wills, at the time 96 years of age, was

showing her younger friend, Mrs. Althea Hood, how, as children, they would carry each other at play with a carriage seat formed by two of them gripping each other's wrists. It was in a spirit of joyful abandon that this demonstration took place in the corridor. These two ladies were totally unaware of my presence behind them. In those moments, I discerned a connection between the eucharistic celebration, just completed, and the attitude they exhibited of being caught up in the timeless happiness of the child's world of play.

3. A resident came into my office who had been going through a successful recuperation from surgery. She had lived at Holly Hall for less than a year. She said, "I thank God for Holly Hall . for the room blessing and the acceptance that I have experienced." She continued, "You know, just before they put me to sleep, I thought about the room blessing and those who were with you that day just after I had moved into Holly Hall. It gave me a feeling of peace in my heart."

Notes

1. Dylan Thomas, *The Collected Poems of Dylan Thomas,* (New Directions Books, New York: 1939) p. 128.

2. Paul Tournier, *The Meaning of Gifts* (SCM Press, Ltd., London: 1964) p. 63.

3. William Butler Yeats, *The Collected Poems of William Butler Yeats* (Macmillan Co., New York: 1933) p. 191.

4. Albert C. Outler, *Who Speaks for God* (New York, Oxford University Press: 1968) p. 82.

5. Paul Hoon, *The Integrity of Worship* (Abingdon Press, Nashville: 1971). A discussion of this idea is developed in the Chapter "The Relevance and Irrelevance of Worship," pp. 149-191.

6. Gustavo Gutierrez, translated from the Spanish by Robert M. Barr, *The Power of the Poor in History* (New York, Orbis Books: 1983) p. 38.

7. Stanley Hauerwas, Seminar offered by Duke Divinity School, "Holy Living and Holy Dying," Lake Junaluska, North Carolina; June, 1986.

8. *The Literature of England, An Anthology and History*, Vol. Two, edited by Woods, Watt and Anderson (Scott, Foresman & Company, Chicago: 1936), Robert Browning, "Rabbi Ben Ezra," p. 756.